the adopter's handbook

information resources services

Amy Neil Salter

Updated by Elaine Dibben

Published by
CoramBAAF Adoption and Fostering Academy
41 Brunswick Square
London WC1N 1AZ
www.corambaaf.org.uk

Coram Academy Limited, registered as a company limited by guarantee
in England and Wales number 9697712, part of the Coram group, charity
number 312278

© Amy Neil Salter, 2002, 2004, 2006, 2012, 2013.
Originally published by BAAF

This edition published by CoramBAAF 2018
© Amy Neil Salter, 2018

British Library Cataloguing in Publication Data
A catalogue record for this book is available from the British Library

ISBN 978 1 910039 66 3

Designed by Helen Joubert Design

Printed in Great Britain by The Lavenham Press

Trade distribution by Turnaround Publisher Services, Unit 3, Olympia
Trading Estate, Coburg Road, London N22 6TZ

✉ For the latest news on CoramBAAF titles and special offers, sign up to
our free publications bulletin at https://corambaaf.org.uk/subscribe.

Contents

Introduction   1

1   **Adoption: your questions answered**   5
The children   6
Is adoption right for you?   9
How does the adoption process work?   11
Who can adopt?   16
What is concurrent planning?   20
What is Fostering for Adoption (FfA)?   20
A detailed look at the process for adopters   21
Intercountry adoptions   52

2   **Legal and financial matters**   57
Introduction   58
Summary of the legal entitlements and legal requirements of people involved
in the adoption process   64
The role of the courts in the adoption process   69
Money matters   75

3   **Schooling and education**   83
Introduction   84
What are we entitled to know about our child's educational history?   84
How do I choose a good school for my child?   89
What are "special educational needs and disabilities"?   89
Education, Health and Care Plans   90
Understanding your child's entitlements to special education provision   91

4   **Your child: physical and emotional needs**   97
Introduction   98
Possible effects of neglect and/or abuse on children   98
Obtaining health services for your child   105

5   **For adoptive parents**   117
Introduction   118
Adoptive parents' needs are important too   118
Feelings adoptive parents commonly encounter throughout the adoption experience   119
Attending to the importance of your couple relationship   127
Adoption support   128
Helping yourself and helping your child   131

Appendices   133
Appendix 1: Books, journals and magazines   134
Appendix 2: Organisations, government agencies, websites   141
Appendix 3: National Minimum Standards   150
Appendix 4: The Adoption Passport   153

Index   155

Acknowledgements

Several people have helped make this guide what it is. Useful information has been supplied and sections and draft of the guide have been reviewed by many professionals and experienced parents involved in adoption. I am grateful for their input, advice and guidance. Thanks to members of Adoption UK, who completed the initial questionnaire which sparked this process, and to the following people for their comments on parts or all of the original draft: Hedi Argent, Daphne Batty, Miranda Davies, Lynda Gilbert, Gill Haworth, Marion Hundleby, Mary Lane, Jenifer Lord, Philly Morrall, Shaila Shah, John Simmonds and Justin Simon. Katrina Wilson and Florence Merredew supplied helpful information for the second edition.

About the author

Amy Neil Salter has had a personal involvement with adoption and is a freelance medical writer by profession. She is currently a practising psychotherapist at a community mental health centre in the USA.

This book is dedicated to her parents, who taught her everything.

Updated editions

Several previous editions of this book were updated by Jenifer Lord, who was for many years a Child Placement Consultant for BAAF. This edition has been updated by Elaine Dibben, who is CoramBAAF's Adoption Development Consultant and who has authored several books on adoption and related subjects.

Some material in Chapter 5 has been provided by Damian McCann D.Psy.Syst. Head of Learning and Development, Couple Psychoanalytic Psychotherapist & Clinical Lecturer, at Tavistock Relationships. For more information on Tavistock Relationships and the services they offer, visit: www.tavistockrelationships.org.

Foreword

We become adopters for a huge range of reasons. Infertility, the wish to help a child, a drive to expand our families, because adoption has featured in our own lives – any combination of these and many other motivations lie behind the decision to parent a child not born with our genes.

As we move along our adoption journeys, we quickly discover an enormous volume of information – anecdotes, articles, books and blogs – exploring aspects of adoption. While we're lucky, as a community, to have access to such an array of perspectives, experiences and expertise, it's easy to become confused and overwhelmed. What adopters need is a go-to source of clear, practical information about the adoption system.

The Adopter's Handbook is that source. It provides a crisp, factual guide to everything you need to know before, during and after the adoption process. From whether adoption is the right choice for you, to considerations around approval and matching, with chapters on financial and legal matters, schools and education, and adopted children's development and health needs, the handbook is packed with accessible and comprehensive explanations of processes, issues and sources of help. Richly signposted with links to additional resources, *The Adopter's Handbook* cleverly strings together all of the stages, questions and guidance connected to adoption, without getting bogged down in any of them.

But it isn't all PARs and panels. *The Adopter's Handbook* recognises that this is a human process, fraught with hopes, fears, doubts and excitement – for adopters and children alike. Now in its sixth edition, it has been updated to reflect developments in policy and practice, with a new chapter on adoption support for both children and adopters – including the all-important need for self-care for adoptive parents. We can't absorb and heal the trauma our children have suffered without taking the time to look after ourselves.

The majority of children adopted today are placed from care. Many of them will have suffered abuse and neglect, and none will have experienced the continuity of care and love that all children need and should have. These are among the most vulnerable children in our society. Adoption is an opportunity to transform these children's lives, breaking what can sometimes be a generations-long cycle of dysfunction, offering them the stability and encouragement to become all that they can be.

Around 4,000 children will be adopted this year in England. All of them deserve adoptive parents who will love and support them to overcome the trauma of their pasts. They need us to be the best parents we can be, well-supported with information, guidance and practical help, an understanding of our rights, and equipped with the knowledge we need to secure a bright future for our children, as well as ourselves.

The Adopter's Handbook provides a much-needed roadmap for our adoption journeys. Whatever our reasons to adopt, and whatever the unique and wonderful children we parent, we will all benefit from this beautifully complete and transparent explanation of how the adoption system works.

Dr Sue Armstrong Brown
Chief Executive, Adoption UK
September 2018

Introduction

Why a guide?

ADOPTING A CHILD is a "human" process – indeed, a "life" process. It is a process in which adults commit themselves to bringing a child into their home, to love and to nurture, and most importantly, to meet the specific needs of that child. Yet adoption is also a service provided by your local authority or by an adoption agency. As adopters, therefore, you are active participants in that service, and it is in your best interest to know as much as possible about the process of adoption and about the wider issues that may affect you and your family along the way.

The purpose of this guide is to help you to help yourself throughout the adoption process and beyond. So, you may be interested to read this information for any of the following reasons:

Because adoption has changed: Adoption and fostering of children in England, Wales and Scotland has undergone immense change in the last decades. There has been continuing interest in adoption from the government, the press, and from the parents and professionals involved so closely in the adoption process. There is, consequently, a need for accurate, precise information about adoption *before, during* and *after* the "big" event.

Because being informed and aware helps avoid misunderstandings and needless stress: If you know what to expect along the way – for example, the expectations of social workers, the length of time involved, and the potential needs of the child – you will be better able to handle the potential ups and downs of the adoption experience. "Forewarned is forearmed" has never been more true than with adoption – the more you know, the less likely you are to be "surprised" by various events.

Because you will need support and information throughout the adoption process and beyond: If you're just starting on the road to adoption, you'll find that certain aspects of adoption practice may vary from region to region. Use this guide to give you a general understanding of adoption, while asking your social worker to inform you of specific issues after the adoption – when the initial joys of adopting a child have receded and the parents suddenly are left with "real life" issues to face. Use this guide to point yourself in the right direction to find the information and services that can help you build your own framework of support – as much or as little as you need.

Because you want to help your child: During and after adoption, you may suddenly find you need information from a variety of sources – medical, psychological and educational, for instance. You suddenly need to become "expert" in many areas and need to know how to access the systems and services available to you. There is a wealth of information available. The purpose of this guide is to present it between two covers, so you can seek appropriate information and access to services quickly and easily.

Because you are a "consumer" of adoption services: It is, therefore, in your best interests to have a general awareness of the laws, regulations and practice guidelines that affect adoption services provided by local authorities and registered voluntary agencies. Knowledge of these will enable you to ensure the service you receive is of the highest possible quality. It will also enable you to take action if you believe you are not receiving an adequate service.

Although you are being assessed throughout most of the adoption process, you must also feel free to express your own opinions and feelings – even when they differ from those of your social worker, local authority or adoption agency. This guide provides details of the adoption services you should expect to receive, your rights throughout the adoption process, and where to find help if you have a question or complaint about these services, rights or procedures.

Who is this guide for?

There are many people involved in the adoption process. If the adoption experience has touched your life in any way, then this guide is for you as well as for:

- **adoptive parents** who adopted years ago, but who continue to confront issues and want to find the best help available for their children;

- **prospective adopters** just beginning the adoption process – use this guide as your "road map" throughout the adoption and, later, as backup information as the adoption proceeds;

- **social care professionals** who want to know what adoptive parents and prospective adopters really think and what they really want to know;

- **anyone adopted as a child** and who is seeking information and support;

- **everyone involved with the issues of adoption** or who interacts with adopted children – teachers, mental health professionals, medical professionals, education authorities.

When you have finished using this guide, pass it on to someone else. The more people who are aware of adoption and the issues involved, the easier it will be for our adopted children to live in a community that understands, and is sensitive to, their needs.

Please note that this guide is primarily for readers in England as the legislative framework, processes and procedures described here pertain to law in England. However, in many cases, resources throughout the UK are listed, i.e. organisations and support networks in England, Wales, Scotland and some in Northern Ireland. We hope that this will be helpful to our readers.

How to use this guide

This guide is divided into five sections, based on *topics identified by adoptive parents.* Each section is organised according to questions adopters commonly ask. Each section also includes the following standard features:

- **A list of specific topics** covered in the section: this gives you a brief overview of the section so you may determine if it contains the information you're seeking;

- **Terms you may need to know** that are used in adoption, and may be unfamiliar;

- **Helpful resources:** books, information, organisations and services that can help you to help yourself in meeting your and your child's needs;

- Also included are **brief descriptions of current programmes, new initiatives, services and legislation** that enable you to be an informed "consumer" of adoption services. This information is not intended to provide a basis for antagonism. It is provided in the spirit of "informed co-operation" – to enable you to work co-operatively with everyone involved in the adoption process.

In addition, this guide includes four **appendices** for quick, easy access to books and magazines (Appendix 1); the useful organisations and resources mentioned in each section (Appendix 2); and relevant sections from the National Minimum Standards for adoption and statutory Adoption Guidance for England (Appendix 3), and Adoption Passport (Appendix 4). Lastly, an **index** is included.

The information in each section is presented in a *quick reference format,* so you can:

- look up information when you need it – there is no need to read the entire guide at once; and

- look for information to meet your specific needs – all children and families differ, so your concerns and needs will also differ. There is no need to read through information that does not apply to you.

This sixth edition has been comprehensively updated. It includes information from the Children and Families Act 2014, Children and Social Work Act 2017, Care Planning, Placement and Review Regulations 2015, Adoption Minimum Standards (NMS) 2011, and draft Adoption Guidance 2014 for England.

Note: We have done our best to ensure that details for the organisations listed are correct. However, as we all know, organisations move, change their names, or even close down. Thankfully, the internet makes checking and tracking down services much easier than before; most of the organisations listed now have websites, which they didn't when the guide was first published.

Adoption: your questions answered

1

In this section:

→ gain an overview of the adoption process and of the points to consider before proceeding with adoption

→ discover how the adoption process works and how to work effectively with everyone involved in that process

→ find out who can or cannot adopt and what factors are important

→ learn about intercountry adoption and about specific issues that may affect this

The children

In the four countries of the UK, there are currently around 96,500 children looked after by local authorities. Numbers have risen steadily over the last few years. Being "in care" or being "looked after" means that most of these children are not living with their birth parent/s, but are living in foster care or in community homes. Many of these children will eventually return to their birth family, some of them after a relatively short time. However, some of these children are waiting to be adopted. In recent years, between 3,000–5,000 children have been adopted annually who were looked after, i.e. in the care of the local authority, before being adopted.

All sorts of children need adoption. These include babies, toddlers and school-age children; groups of brothers and sisters who want to stay together; disabled children; children with learning disabilities; children from different minority ethnic communities – all these children can benefit tremendously from family life. We estimate that there are currently about 2,000 children waiting to be adopted.

Although it is in the child's – and everyone's – best interests to remain with his or her birth family whenever possible, adoption may be recommended as one of a range of options for permanence when the child's welfare is considered to be at risk if the child returns to or remains with the birth family.

The European Court of Human Rights considers the relationship between birth parent/s and child to be 'a fundamental aspect of family life that is not terminated when a child is placed in care'. A local authority's decision to remove a child from the birth family must, therefore, be based on reasons that comply with the European Convention on Human Rights.

How does a child come to need to be adopted?

Figure 1 shows the general process by which children become looked after by a local authority and may be placed for adoption. A general knowledge of this process can help adoptive parents understand the experiences of their child becoming looked after, the time periods involved in each stage of the process, and the attempts by local authorities to rehabilitate the child with the birth family.

When is foster care, rather than adoption, considered best for a child?

Children's services departments will consider long-term fostering, a child arrangements order or a special guardianship order for a child if it believes the child will benefit from continued involvement with the birth family, or if the child is older and does not wish to be adopted. In some cases, a child's sense of identity and self-esteem may be strongly connected to the birth family, but his or her additional needs require that he or she be fostered or cared for under a child arrangements order or a special guardianship order. Long-term foster arrangements, child arrangements orders or special guardianship orders may also be considered if the child's birth parents are able and willing to continue to exercise some degree of parental responsibility for the child.

Adoption is considered for the child if the local authority has assessed that the child's needs – physical, emotional and developmental – cannot be met by the birth parents or by any other family members. In order for these needs to be met, the child needs to be placed in a new family that is in a legal position to commit themselves to the child emotionally, socially and legally throughout childhood and beyond as the child's legal parents.

Figure 1 **Routes by which a child becomes looked after and potentially is placed for adoption**

Child relinquished for adoption by birth parents

Looked after children

```
Adoption requested by parents.
        ↓
Statutory counselling of parents.
        ↓                    ↓
```

Child under six weeks of age
Birth parents agree to adoptive placement in writing with agency.

Child over six weeks of age
Birth parents sign section 19 consent to placement for adoption witnessed by CAFCASS officer.

Adoption panel recommendation and agency decision that child should be placed for adoption.
        ↓
Parents notified. Child matched with prospective adopters and placed for adoption.

Birth parent/s in contact with local authority (LA) – self-referral or via GP, school, health visitor, etc.
        ↓   ↓
Assessment of child's needs and whether they are being met or could be met by birth family, incl. extended family.

Emergency protection order or police protection powers and child removed.
        ↓
Work with family to enable them to parent child adequately.
        ↓
Child returned home.   ←   Help offered including respite foster care or placement with relatives.
        ↓
Case conference/review decision that child should be removed from home or remain in foster care. Parents agree.
        ↓
A review agrees that the option for permanence is return home or kinship care, fostering or special guardianship, etc.   ←   Assessment of child's needs. Review at four months agrees a permanence plan – adoption is one of a range of options including return home, kinship placement, foster care or special guardianship.
        ↓
Parents consent to adoption. Case referred to adoption panel 'should be placed for adoption' recommendation.   ←   LA decides that adoption is the preferred option for permanence. Parents notified.
        ↓   ↓
Parent(s) agree and sign section 19 consent.

Parents do not agree but LA decides that the child should be placed for adoption.
        ↓
Adoption care plan submitted to court in the care proceedings and LA applies for placement order.
        ↓
Child matched with prospective adopters and placed for adoption.   ←   Care order and placement order granted.

Reproduced (with amendments) from *Effective Adoption Panels,* 7th edn., CoramBAAF, 2016.

Is adoption right for you?

Clearly, there are many children who need a loving and secure home, and many more people are needed to be adoptive parents. But this doesn't *necessarily* mean adoption is the right choice for everyone. It is important to consider in a clear and logical manner your decision to adopt – to avoid the temptation to be led to your decision purely by emotion.

The fact that you are reading this guide means you are investigating the option of adopting children. You and your family may have discussed many of the different issues involved already. But if you don't know much about adoption, or don't know anyone who has adopted children, you might want to think about some of the following questions.

Why do I/we want to adopt?

We cannot escape the fact that deciding to have children, through birth or through adoption, fulfils some of our own needs and desires to become parents and to raise a family. After all, this is a natural process in life. Yet most children waiting for adoption have specific emotional and physical needs (see Section 4 for more explanation) and require parents who can commit to being with them through good times and through tough times. The process of adoption, therefore, must necessarily focus on the *child's* needs and on meeting those needs as much as possible.

When you begin the process of adoption, you must also be willing to address your own emotional needs (for example, attachment issues from your own childhood, infertility issues, grief over a lost child, etc.) and must be sure that adoption is not simply a route to overcome your own difficulties.

Is parenting an adopted child different from parenting my own birth child?

Yes. Most children who are placed for adoption have experienced some degree of abuse and/or neglect. And all children needing adoption suffer the trauma of separation from, and loss of, their birth family. These events affect children of *all* ages (even babies) and in many different ways (see Section 4 for more information about these effects). While most children are able to "recover" from their experiences when placed in a loving environment, it is important to understand that the road to recovery can be difficult and frustrating for both the child and the adoptive parents.

It is also important to understand that older children (age 3+), especially, will have begun to develop their own personality and habits by the time they are adopted. As parents, your personality and habits will still influence the child, but less so than if the child had been born to you.

9

Is it "easier" to parent an older child or a younger child?

Research* has shown that there is a low rate of adoptions that don't work out – around three per cent. For children placed for adoption over four years of age this may be a risk factor, but there is no guarantee that a younger child will have fewer difficulties than an older child. Even babies can suffer the effects of early trauma or neglect (see Section 4). Only you can decide what age child you want to adopt. The most important consideration is to determine how you can best meet the needs of that child.

Can children who have experienced trauma, abuse and/or neglect ever overcome these experiences?

Yes. Section 4 of this guide describes the many complex emotional, developmental and physical difficulties children can experience as a result of abuse and/or neglect. In some cases, such experiences can affect the physical growth and development of neural connections in the brain and thus affect the child's emotions and behaviour. Studies[†] have shown that, with appropriate treatment (medical, psychiatric and/or psychological), these neural connections can form – the brain can be helped to adapt to compensate for earlier neglect.

When considering adoption, the two key things to remember are:

- providing a loving and secure home will help the child, but may not help the child resolve *all* of his or her problems – you may have to seek additional assistance from a variety of sources; and

- the wounds of abuse and neglect run deep – even if the child was removed from the abusive environment at an early age.

As adoptive parents, therefore, we must look realistically at our own expectations of our child and his or her "recovery". It may take many years (perhaps a lifetime) for the child to overcome the complex effects of early trauma.

---

[*]   J Selwyn, S Meakings and D Wijedawa, *Beyond the Adoption Order: Challenges, interventions and adoption disruption*, BAAF, 2015.

[†]   J. Selwyn, W. Sturgess, D. Quinton and C. Baxter, *Costs and Outcomes of Non-Infant Adoptions*, BAAF, 2006

HELPFUL BOOKS

For more information and publications about the effects of early trauma, see Section 4 and Appendix 1 of this guide.

Attachment, Trauma and Resilience: Therapeutic caring for children
by Kate and Brian Cairns, CoramBAAF, 2016
Written by a couple who fostered several children over a 25-year period, this book provides an illustration of family life with children who had lived through overwhelming stress and how they were helped to overcome it.

First Steps in Parenting the Child Who Hurts: Tiddlers and toddlers by Caroline Archer, Jessica Kingsley, 1999
This book approaches the attachment and developmental issues that arise when even the youngest child is in your care.

Next Steps in Parenting the Child Who Hurts: Tykes and teens by Caroline Archer, Jessica Kingsley, 1999
This book follows on logically from the *First Steps* book and continues into the challenging journey through childhood and into adolescence.

The Primal Wound: Understanding the adopted child by Nancy Verrier, BAAF, 2009 (UK edn)
This book contains profound insights and revelations on what being adopted means to adopted people. The book explores the "primal wound" that results when a child is separated from his or her mother and the trauma it can cause.

Coming Home to Self: Healing the primal wound by Nancy Verrier, BAAF, 2010 (UK edn)
Considers the effects of separation trauma on brain development and explores some of the most troubling emotions and examines ways of healing and achieving meaningful relationships and personal power.

Loving and Living with Traumatised Children by Megan Hirst, BAAF, 2005
Looks at the experience of adopting traumatised children and the effects this can have on their carers and adoptive parents, based on the experiences of nine individuals.

How does the adoption process work?

Getting started

You can get useful general information from First4Adoption, an information service on adoption in England (www.first4adoption.org.uk), the National Adoption Service in Wales (www.adoptcymru.com) or from Adoption UK – a UK-wide self-help organisation for adoptive and prospective adoptive parents (www.adoptionuk.org).

Once you have decided you are interested in adopting a child, the first step is to contact a local authority's adoption team or a voluntary adoption agency to ask for information and procedures. These usually cover geographical areas and are all listed on the First4Adoption website.

If you are interested in adopting a specific child you have seen in a family-finding publication or website: you should contact the organisation that produces the publication/website for information and then the local authority looking after the child. Link Maker and Adoption Match are two national family-finding services.

When you contact an adoption agency: you will receive written information and you will be offered a follow-up interview with a social worker and/or an invitation to an information meeting, or a pre-planned phone call. This will give you the opportunity to find out more about adoption and about the waiting children, to ask questions and to talk a bit about your hopes and plans. This should happen within 10 days of your initial enquiry to the agency. If, after this, you decide to proceed, you will need to formally register your interest in doing so. The agency will provide you with a Registration of Interest form with which to do this.

The key players

There are five key players in the adoption process:

- the child;
- the local authority adoption team OR the voluntary adoption agency which has assessed you, your assessing social worker and team manager;
- the local authority which is responsible for the child (which may or may not be the same one as above), the child's social worker and team manager;
- you, the prospective adoptive parent/s; and
- the birth parent(s) or child's legal guardians.

The courts also play a role in the adoption process, at different points along the way.

Voluntary adoption agencies

Voluntary adoption agencies are usually smaller agencies than local authorities. They work to the same regulations, guidance and national minimum standards as local authorities. They recruit, assess, approve and support adoptive parents who will have children looked after by a local authority placed with them.

Social workers

All social workers in the UK are required to have a qualification approved by the Health and Care Professions Council (HCPC) or equivalent body. They are required to be registered with these bodies. The qualification involves a minimum of three years' training, culminating in a degree.

The following organisations are involved in the development and management of the social care industry:

- **Health and Care Professions Council** (HCPC)

- **Ofsted** (Office for Standards in Education, Children's Services and Skills)

- **Department for Education** (DfE)

- **Social Care Institute for Excellence** (SCIE) collects and synthesises up-to-date knowledge about what works in social care and makes that widely available.

National Minimum Standards are in force to specify how adoption and fostering services should be delivered. Adoption services are inspected every three years against these Standards (see Appendix 3). The DfE publishes guidance – statutory and practice guidance – which shapes the way that adoption and fostering services are provided.

Figure 2 shows a *general* flowchart of the route to adoption of a child, as seen by the local authority. Below, we look in detail at the adoption process for prospective adopters.

How can I prepare for adoption?

No one can ever be fully "prepared" for the adoption process and for the eventual arrival of a child in their home. But there are things you can do to make the process a bit easier and to "initially" prepare yourself as much as possible to meet the needs of the child who may become a part of your family.

- Once you tell an agency about your interest in adoption, you will be given written and verbal information. When you have applied to the agency you will be given preparation, which may be by attendance at groups. You will have a chance to explore a range of issues about adoption and children's needs. You can read *Preparing to Adopt* (the Workbook), part of a training guide published by CoramBAAF, and watch the accompanying DVD (Appendix 1).

- You can access the e-learning material on the First4Adoption website – www.first4adoption.org.uk.

- You can read about the adoption process, so you understand the functions and responsibilities of everyone involved – this helps avoid misunderstandings. *Adopting a Child*, a popular guide published by

Figure 2 **Process for identifying a family after a decision that a child should be placed for adoption**

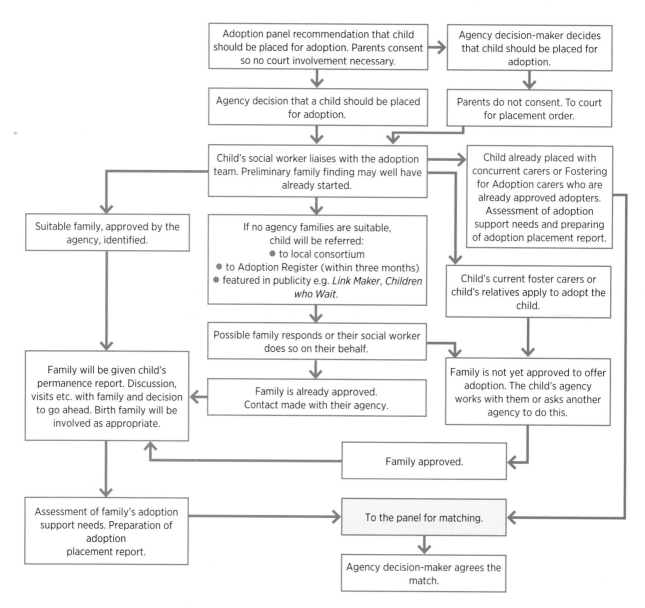

Reproduced (with amendments) from *Effective Adoption Panels,* 7th edn., CoramBAAF, 2016.

CoramBAAF and regularly revised (most recently in 2016), provides a comprehensive account.

- You can gain experience of other people's children, e.g. attend Parentcraft classes at your local clinic or hospital, or volunteer to help at your local school, play group or nursery.

- You can meet adoptive parents, through joining Adoption UK.

- If you are a lesbian or gay adopter, you can meet others through joining New Family Social.

- You can read about and be aware of the impact of trauma and neglect on children of all ages.

HELPFUL ORGANISATIONS

General information about adoption

Adoption UK
A UK-wide support organisation for adoptive parents and prospective adopters with local groups and messageboards. Also publishes a monthly magazine, *Adoption Today*, with news, views and features, and a supplement and website, *Children Who Wait*, which features children needing adoption.

Units 11 and 12, Vantage Business Park,
Bloxham Road, Banbury, Oxfordshire
OX16 9UX
Helpline: 07904 793974
www.adoptionuk.org

CoramBAAF
Provides up-to-date information about all aspects of adoption on the website and in useful pamphlets and guides, including *Adopting a Child*.

41 Brunswick Square
London WC1N 1AZ
Tel: 020 7520 0300
www.corambaaf.org.uk

Department for Education
The government department responsible for adoption and fostering services and for other services to children and families.

Tel: 0370 000 2288
**www.education.gov.uk/
childrenandyoungpeople/families/
adoption**

New Family Social is a UK charity for lesbian, gay, bisexual and transgender adopters, foster carers and their children. It provides advice and information, a vibrant messageboard, as well as social events for parents and children to get together.

Harvey's Barn
Park End
Swaffham
Bulbeck CB25 0NA
Tel: 0843 289 9457
www.newfamilysocial.org.uk

First4Adoption is an information service for people interested in adopting a child from England. Information line open 10am–6pm Monday–Friday.

Tel: 0300 222 0022
www.first4adoption.org.uk

Link Maker is a social enterprise aiming to help match children with prospective adopters and foster carers. The website also provides an online community for prospective adopters and those who have adopted, with message boards, advice, support and a "playdate finder".

St Nicholas House
31–34 High Street
Bristol BS1 2AW
Tel: 0843 886 0040
www.linkmaker.co.uk

Adoption Match is a national service working to match children needing adoption with prospective adopters. It manages the Adoption Register for England, and provides adoption exchange days and adoption activity days. The website provides information about adoption and prospective adopters can submit a profile to be entered into the Adoption Register to be considered for matches.

Adopter helpline: 0345 222 9058
www.adoptionmatch.org.uk

- You can read about the experiences of others who have adopted (see booklist).

  It is impossible to prepare yourself for every aspect of the adoption process, because you can't anticipate everything that may occur. The best preparation is to read about the adoption process and about the children as you go along, so you will know how to access help right away, if you need it.

Who can adopt?

Almost anyone can apply to be an adoptive parent if they can show that they can provide a loving, secure home that will meet the needs of a particular child.

Adoption Guidance makes clear that no one can be denied the opportunity to be considered as an adoptive parent because of their ethnic background, marital status, sexuality or age. It spells out the eligibility criteria, as follows:

- The prospective adopter(s) is single, married, in a civil partnership or an unmarried couple (same sex or opposite sex) and over 21 years old. (The birth parent in a step-parent adoption must be 18 or older.)

- The prospective adopter or one of them has their permanent home (domicile) in England, Wales, Scotland, Northern Ireland, the Channel Islands, on the Isle of Man, or both members of a couple have been habitually resident there for at least a year before they apply to court for an adoption order.

- Neither prospective adopter nor an adult member of their household has been convicted or cautioned for a specified offence. These are principally offences against children.

What sorts of families can adopt?

Although the majority of adopters are still married couples, all sorts of families can and do adopt very successfully. In fact, research* has found that some family structures, such as single parents, can better meet the needs of particular children (such as those who have been sexually abused or who may need to interact with only one parent).

---

* See B Betts, *A Marginalised Resource? Recruiting, assessing and supporting single carers*, BAAF, 2007, N Hill, *Proud Parents: Lesbian and gay fostering and adoption experiences*, BAAF, 2013, and L. Mellish *et al*, *Gay, Lesbian and Heterosexual Adoptive Families*, BAAF, 2013.

HELPFUL BOOKS

One of the Familly: A handbook for kinship carers, by Hedi Argent, BAAF, 2005
A practical handbook which gives family and friends who may become kinship carers information about the choices they can make, the child care system and the support they can expect.

Becoming Dads by Pablo Fernández, BAAF, 2011
A diarised narrative account of how Pablo and Mike adopt their son.

Flying Solo by Julia Wise, BAAF, 2007
A single parent's adoption story.

Is it True you have Two Mums? by Ruby Clay, BAAF, 2011
Charts the adoption journey of a lesbian couple who adopt three girls.

Loving and Living with Traumatised Children: Reflections by adoptive parents by Megan Hirst, BAAF, 2005
A group of adopters tell of their experiences and the effect on themselves of adopting traumatised children.

Dale's Tale, by Helen Jayne, BAAF, 2010
The story of Helen, a foster carer, and her family, who look after, and then decide to adopt, their young foster child, Dale.

The Pink Guide to Adoption for Lesbians and Gay Men (second edition) by Nicola Hill, BAAF, 2012
A step-by-step guide to adopting, including accounts by those going through the process.

Couples who live together, as well as married or civil registered couples, can adopt jointly.

We should keep in mind that children may have fewer predetermined views about families.

Here are some answers to common questions prospective adopters ask.

We are foster carers and we want to adopt our foster child. How do we do this? If you want to adopt a child whom you are fostering and have the agreement of the local authority, it is best to discuss your wishes with them and, if possible, to go through the adoption process with them. There is a "fast track" for approved foster carers in England who wish to adopt. They can enter the assessment process at Stage Two, which provides for an assessment and decision within four months. If you have fostered a child for at least one year, or longer, you can apply to the court for an adoption order, whether or not the child's local authority agrees. However, you must give notice in writing to the local authority three months before you make the application. If the local authority does not

Figure 3 **Families offering placements – from first enquiry to approval**

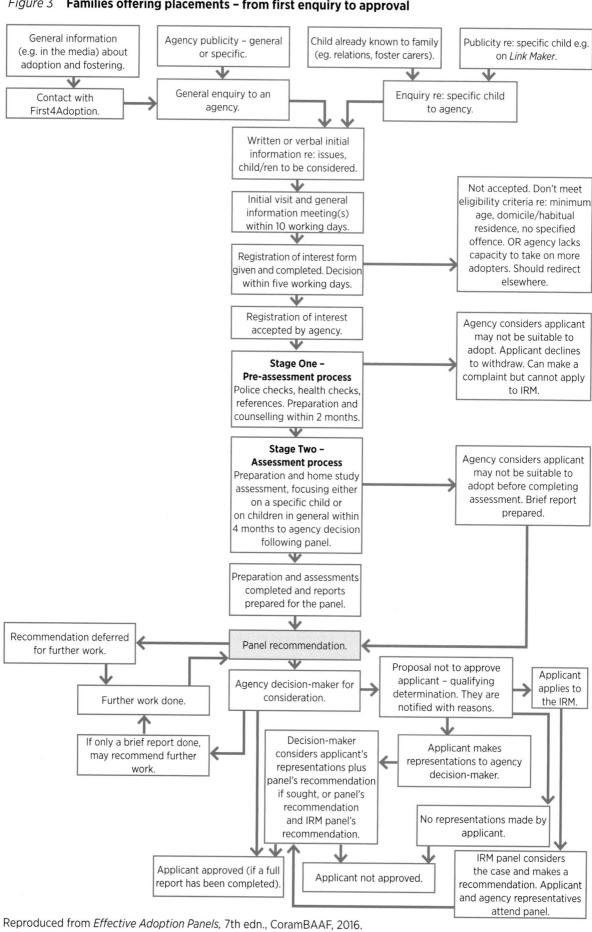

Reproduced from *Effective Adoption Panels,* 7th edn., CoramBAAF, 2016.

agree with your application, you will only be eligible for limited post-adoption support.

We want to adopt our grandchildren. How can we do this? In most cases, it is likely that a child arrangements order or special guardianship order will be the best way for you to provide your grandchildren with permanence, so you should make sure you have all the information you need before deciding the best route for you and the children. As relatives of the children, whether or not they are looked after by the local authority, you can apply to adopt them after the children have lived with you for three years. You can apply to the court for permission to apply sooner than this. You must give written notice to the local authority at least three months before you apply for the adoption order. The court will then decide if the adoption order or any other order, such as a child arrangements order or a special guardianship order, is in the children's best interests. The court will take into account the local authority's views about this. If the children are looked after by the local authority and you are currently fostering them, the answer above in relation to foster carers applies to you.

My husband and I are from different ethnic backgrounds. Will this affect our ability to adopt a child? In fact, there are many children of mixed ethnic backgrounds, so families such as yours are particularly needed.

My partner and I are not married, but we want to adopt a child. Can we do this? Yes. Unmarried couples (lesbian, gay, or heterosexual) or couples who have not entered into a civil partnership, can adopt jointly.

My partner and I are in a same-sex relationship. Can we adopt a child? Yes. Lesbian or gay couples can adopt jointly just as any other couple.

I am a single parent. Can I adopt a child? Yes, single people can adopt. Research has found that some children benefit from placement with a single adult; for example, girls who have been sexually abused, and children who have witnessed severe conflict between parents or those who will benefit from the one-to-one attention and care provided by one adult.

I am in my late 40s and my partner is over 50. Can we adopt? Yes, this could be possible. Adoption Guidance states that older and more experienced adopters could have something special to offer to older children if they enjoy sufficient health and vigour to meet the child's varied demands; it cautions that too large an age gap between adopter and child may have an adverse effect upon the child. Adopters need to be able to meet the many and varied demands of children in their growing years and be there for them into adulthood.

If we had a placement that disrupted, can we apply for adoption again? If you have previously had a child placed with you for adoption and the placement did not work out for you, don't be put off. The adoption agency that originally approved you must undertake a review of your approval. This may be positive, but if not, they must ask their panel to make a recommendation about your continued approval, if the agency is of the view that your approval should be terminated. If the agency proposal is to terminate your approval, you can apply to the Independent Review Mechanism (IRM) for a review of that proposal. You may decide not to remain with the agency that approved you, and instead apply to another agency. It will be important to be honest with a new agency about your previous experience of adoption.

What is concurrent planning?

This is the term given to schemes run by some agencies in which children, usually babies or toddlers, for whom there is a chance that they might return home to their birth family, are placed with families who will foster them with this aim. However, the foster carers are also approved as adopters and will adopt the child should the planned return to the birth family not be successful. In this way, the moves that a child may otherwise have to make are minimised. These schemes have to be run with the agreement and co-operation of the local courts and to tight timescales. Families who have children placed under a concurrency scheme have to be prepared to facilitate very regular contact for the child with their birth family and to be prepared that the child may return home. However, adoption often becomes the plan for these children and the carers can then adopt a child who has been placed with them from a young age. If you might be interested in becoming a carer in a concurrency scheme, There is information and guidance on the website www.earlypermanence. org.uk about concurrent planning and Fostering for Adoption.

What is Fostering for Adoption (FfA)?

The Care Planning, Placement and Case Review and Fostering Services (Miscellaneous Amendments) Regulations 2015 allow an agency to give an approved adopter temporary approval as a foster carer for a named child. This enables a child to be placed as a foster child with carers without them having had a full fostering assessment or panel approval as foster carers. These will be children for whom the local authority has decided that adoption is the right plan. However, the child is fostered until, in most cases, work with birth parents and court involvement enables an adoption plan to be agreed and the child to be matched for adoption with these carers at panel. If you might be interested in becoming an FfA carer, you should discuss this with your agency during your assessment.

The children placed in this way are likely to be quite young. However, you must be aware of the uncertainty about the final option as there are a small number of cases where adoption is not agreed as the plan or court involvement takes longer than anticipated.

A detailed look at the process for adopters

Ten steps to becoming an adoptive parent

After you have decided to consider adopting, the main steps of the adoption process for prospective adopters are:

1   You get general information about adoption and have a pre-planned phone call or a meeting with a social worker and/or attend an adoption information meeting. You complete a Registration of Interest form.

2   Your Registration of Interest is accepted and you move on to Stage One of the assessment process. This involves initial counselling, training and preparation, and police checks, health checks and references are undertaken.

3   You notify the agency that you wish to move to Stage Two, which involves an assessment by a social worker of your suitability to adopt a looked after child. You will probably attend more in-depth preparation groups with other prospective adopters.

4   The report written by your social worker about you – the Prospective Adopter's Report (PAR) – is given to an adoption panel for their recommendation of your approval as prospective adopters. The agency decision-maker makes the final decision. If you are also being dually approved as a foster carer for FfA or concurrency, this can happen at the same panel.

5a Once you are approved, if you have been dually approved to foster or have expressed an interest in FfA, you may be asked to consider fostering a child while the court process is being concluded.

5b Once you are approved, the social workers consider a match between you and a child who has been authorised for adoption by a placement order or a section 19 parental consent. The social worker from the child's agency sends you the Child's Permanence Report and arranges to meet you to discuss the proposed match. If it is agreed that the match will proceed, the child's agency must assess your and the child's support needs and agree a support plan with you.

6   An adoption panel considers the proposed match, makes a recommendation and advises on contact, adoption support and exercise of parental responsibilities. The child's local authority then makes a decision to proceed with the match.

7   You and the child are introduced.

8   The child moves in (i.e. is placed with you).

9   An adoption order is made through the court.

10 Settling in, and post-placement and post-adoption support.

Let's look at each of these steps in detail.

1   Initial information gathering

Once you have contacted an adoption agency covering your area, they should respond within ten working days. They should invite you to an information meeting or offer you an individual visit or a pre-planned telephone call. These can take place in the evening or at a weekend if this suits you best. You will be given information on the adoption process and on the parenting needs of the children. This is an opportunity for you to consider whether adoption is likely to be right for you and how adopting a child who may have a range of complex needs will impact on your family. If you decide to proceed to the next stage, you need to complete a Registration of Interest form which the agency will supply. Among other things, this will authorise the agency to undertake the checks described in the next section. It will also confirm that you have not registered with any other agency. The agency should decide within five working days from receipt of your form whether or not to accept it. If the agency lacks the capacity to undertake assessments in the immediate future, it should advise you of this and offer to refer you to another agency.

2   Stage One – the pre-assessment process

This stage begins when the agency accepts your Registration of Interest and should normally take no more than two months to complete. The agency should discuss with you the work which will take place and should complete a written Stage One agreement with you detailing this. It should offer you some initial training and preparation and it must also complete the prescribed checks.

Checks are made of criminal records for you and members of your household aged over 18. Offences other than specified ones, i.e. those against children, need not rule you out, although the nature of the offence and how long ago it occurred will need to be carefully considered. It's vital that you are open and honest. Any attempt at deception will be taken very seriously. These checks are made to the Disclosure and Barring Service (DBS). Checks will also be made of the local authority where you live. You will be asked for the names of at least three personal referees, people who know you really well, and they will be interviewed. If you have parented children with a previous partner, the agency will want your permission to contact him or her. They may want to talk to adult children whom you've parented. They will want to check that you are not seriously in debt and

HELPFUL BOOKS

Adopting a Child by Jenifer Lord, CoramBAAF, 2016
This popular guide describes what adoption means and how to go about it, including procedures and practices, legal requirements, the costs involved and support available.

Our Adoption Journey, by Jayne Lilley, CoramBAAF, 2016
A true story of an adoption which tracks Jayne, Dan and their son Charlie through the adoption process, and to their adoption of Jessie, a baby girl.

Guiding you Through the Adoption Process available from Adoption UK, last revised 2015
Provides a comprehensive step-by-step guide through the adoption process.

that payments on your home are up to date. Finally, you will need a full medical examination carried out by your GP. This will be considered by the adoption agency's medical adviser.

If the agency decides during or at the end of Stage One that you are not suitable to adopt, it must inform you in writing with clear reasons. You may make a complaint to the agency about this. However, you are not able to apply to the Independent Review Mechanism. You may, if you wish, take a break of up to a maximum of six months after Stage One, or you may notify the agency that you wish to proceed straight to Stage Two.

3 Stage Two – the assessment process

This stage starts when the agency receives notification from you that you wish to proceed with the assessment process. It finishes with the agency decision about your suitability as an adopter and should normally be completed within four months. A Stage Two written assessment plan must be completed with you, detailing the assessment process, dates for meetings and agreed training. The social worker designated to work with you will visit you at your home. The purpose of these visits is for the social worker to gain a detailed view of you and other family members in the home, in order to assess your suitability to adopt a child.The social worker will want to talk with your children, both those at home and usually with adult children living elsewhere. They will usually also want to meet any ex-partner with whom you have parented children. They may well want to talk further with your referees, although they will have had contact with them during Stage One of the process.

All adoption agencies are required to provide preparation and training and you will almost certainly be invited to a series of group meetings, either half or full days. You will be with other prospective adopters, usually about eight or ten people. As well as hearing from social workers about adoption and the children waiting, you will usually also hear from experienced adopters, an adopted adult and perhaps from a birth parent whose child has been adopted, about their experiences. You will have the opportunity to ask questions and to reflect on your own life experiences and on the impact of any adopted child on your family and how you will adapt to meet their needs.

The social worker records information on the Prospective Adopter's Report (PAR). The Prospective Adopter's Report will include a summary of the medical information about you from your GP.

Working effectively with your social worker

The goal of visits is to assess whether you are suitable to adopt and prepare you for it. Although you may feel uneasy and think the questioning and form-filling too intrusive and detailed, it is best to try to approach these visits with a relaxed, informal attitude. Open, honest communication throughout will help your social worker provide accurate information to the adoption panel. Remember that the social worker needs to ensure not only your parenting skills and capacity, and match these against a particular child or children, but also that any prospective adopter meets the legal requirements (see Section 2).

Why do adoptive parents have to be "assessed" for parenthood, when people giving birth do not? Simply because the purpose of adoption is to focus on the needs of a particular child who has had to be separated from his or her birth family – a child who is already born, with his or her own developing personality, habits and physical and emotional needs. The task of parenting a child not born to you is different and needs to be recognised as such. The social worker's role is to ensure the child's needs are matched as closely as possible to parents who can meet those needs.

YOUR RIGHTS DURING THE ASSESSMENT PROCESS

The Adoption Guidance 2013 and National Minimum Standards 2011 require that:

- Prospective adopters 'are treated fairly, without prejudice, openly and with respect. They are kept informed, on a regular basis, of the progress (or lack of progress) of their enquiry/application.' NMS 10.2

- The agency's decision about the suitability of the prospective adopter to adopt a child should be made within six months of the receipt of the Registration of Interest form. Guidance 3.24–3.52

You should be given a copy of your Prospective Adopter's Report and you are given five working days to comment upon its contents before the panel meets to consider it.

Brief report

If the agency has concerns about your suitability as a prospective adoptive parent, it should discuss these with you. However, if they are unable to be resolved it may decide to halt the process and prepare a brief report. This is presented to the adoption panel which makes a recommendation to the agency. The decision-maker in the agency can then require the agency to complete the assessment or can take the view that you are not suitable to adopt. If this is the case, you have the same rights as if the process had been completed, i.e. to make representations to the agency or to apply to the IRM – see p29.

If you have any questions or concerns which you feel unable to discuss with your social worker, or if you have particular difficulties with the assessment process or with your social worker, you should contact your social worker's manager, or the director of the adoption agency. As a very last resort, you could contact your local councillor or Member of Parliament. You may also contact:

Ofsted (Office for Standards in Education, Children's Services and Skills). It has responsibility for the reputation and inspection of all children's services. Adoption and fostering services must be inspected at least three-yearly.

Piccadilly Gate, Store Street
Manchester M1 2WD
Email: enquiries@ofsted.gov.uk
Tel: 0300 123 1231

Health and Care Professions Council, a regulatory body which sets national standards and registers people working in the health and care professions, including social workers.

Park House, 184 Kennington Park Road, London SE11 4BU
Tel: 0300 500 6184
www.hpc-uk.org

Equivalent bodies for other countries in the United Kingdom include:

- **Social Care Wales** www.socialcare.wales

- **Northern Ireland Social Care Council (NISCC)** www.niscc.info

- **Scottish Social Services Council (SSSC)** www.sssc.uk.com

· ·

4 Your Prospective Adopter's Report (PAR) is given to an adoption panel which makes a recommendation to the agency

When your home study is completed, your social worker will submit your Prospective Adopters' Report to the local authority or voluntary agency's

HELPFUL BOOKS

Effective Adoption Panels (7th edn.) by Jenifer Lord and Deborah Cullen, CoramBAAF, 2016
Primarily aimed at adoption workers and panel members. Full of information about the roles and responsibilities of panel members.

Effective Adoption and Fostering Panels in Scotland by Marjorie Morrison, CoramBAAF, 2018 (new edition forthcoming)
A guide for social workers and panel members on the operation of panels in Scotland.

Prospective Adopters Attending Adoption Panel by Jenifer Lord, CoramBAAF, 2016 (3rd edn.)
Guidance for panel members on the prospective adopters' role at panel, the input they can have, and how to evaluate their contribution.

adoption panel. The **adoption panel** is an advisory group, established by the adoption agency or by the local authority, which:

- considers applications to be approved as adopters (either domestic or intercountry);

- recommends whether or not it believes the prospective applicant/s can meet the needs of a child and, therefore;

- recommends whether or not the applicants should be approved as adoptive parents.

The panel also makes recommendations regarding other aspects of the adoption process, such as whether a child whose parents consent should be placed for adoption and matches between children and adopters. Adoption panels can also advise about support and contact plans and the exercise of parental responsibilities by prospective adopters during placement.

Who is on the adoption panel?

The panel usually consists of about five to seven people, including:

- the Chair – a person who has experience in adoption work and is independent of the agency

- one social worker with experience of adoption

- sometimes a member of the agency's management committee or local authority's social services committee

- usually the medical adviser

- some "independent" persons who are not members or employees of the agency or local authority. Where possible these people should include people with personal experience of adoption.

A panel is only quorate when at least five of its members are present, and this must include the Chair or Vice-chair, a social worker and at least one independent member if the Vice-chair is chairing and not independent. Adoption Agencies Regulations require that applicants be invited to attend the panel meeting.

The composition, terms of reference and functions of an adoption panel are set out in the Adoption Agencies Regulations 2005, the Adoption Agencies and Independent Review of Determinations (Amendment) Regulations 2011, the Adoption Agencies (Panel and Consequential Amendments) Regulations 2012, the Adoption Agencies (Miscellaneous Amendments) Regulations 2013, and statutory Adoption Guidance 2011, revised in 2013.

What issues will the panel consider when considering the application?

The panel will consider the Prospective Adopter's Report provided by your social worker, as well as information about your statutory eligibility and suitability (including marital status, nationality, domicile, criminal records, and financial considerations). Within this context, panel members will focus on the following specific issues.

- **Your reasons for adopting** – panel members will want to be sure that you understand and can address any relevant emotional issues that have led you to adoption.

  For example, why have you applied to adopt? Do you understand your motivation to care for a child? Are you able to identify your own needs and expectations regarding adoption? Have you dealt with issues of infertility (if applicable)?

  This is not to say that you must have resolved all such issues, but that you are able to identify and understand them, and to deal with resulting feelings.

- **The child and birth family** – do you understand the intense emotional needs of children (of any age) who have experienced trauma, separation or loss? What are your feelings regarding the birth parents and their inability to care for the child? Will you be ready to deal with needs that are not yet identified in the child?

- **Your family structure** – do you have a support network you can rely on? Are there other children in the family? The child's position in the family can affect his or her ability to adjust to the family and can be affected by the child's particular emotional needs. Also, research has shown that there is a greater risk that the placement will not thrive if the child is placed in a family that has other children close to him or her in age.

- **Your relationships** – if you are divorced or have had previous partnerships, panel members will consider whether or not there is a pattern of relationship difficulties that could be repeated in the future and, if so, what plans you would then make for the child.

- **Your age** – while law prohibits discrimination on the basis of age, the panel will want to "maximise" the chances that you will remain fit and healthy well into the child's young adulthood. In order to adopt, you must be at least 21 years old.

- **Your current health** – lifestyle and medical issues will be considered for their impact on you and your family. If you have particular concerns, it is best to talk to your social worker about them.

- **If you have a criminal record** – See *Who Can Adopt?,* p16.

The panel will also consider issues of culture, "race" and ethnicity; contact with the birth family; financial requirements (e.g. financial support before and after adoption, financial support [see Section 2]); and requirements for other adoption support.

The panel makes a recommendation, which you will usually be told about immediately. It may also give advice to the agency about the range of your approval, i.e. age range and number of children. The agency's decision should be made within seven working days of receipt of the panel's recommendation and final set of minutes.

5a Dual approval/FfA

If you have been dually approved as a foster carer or are willing to offer FfA, you may be asked to take a child under these arrangements. There may be less information available about the child but you must ensure that you have all the information possible to make the right decision for you. You can find more advice in the leaflet *Fostering for Adoption: A guide for prospective carers* (available at: https://earlypermanence.org.uk/good-practice-guidance/).

5b You are linked and matched with a child

Once you have been approved as suitable to adopt a child, the agency must prepare a written matching agreement with you, setting out the matching process and your role in identifying a possible child for placement with you. It must also refer you, with your agreement, to the Adoption Register immediately, or within three months, unless a link with a specific child is being considered. Your social worker will begin the process of matching you with a child or children and you can be proactive by looking in *Children Who Wait* or on *Link Maker*. In some cases, a child

Your questions answered...

What happens if we're not recommended for approval by the panel?
It is not the panel that will make the final decision but the agency;
the agency is not required to follow the panel's recommendation (see
flowchart on p18).

**What happens if we're not approved by the local authority or the
agency?** If the agency or local authority proposes not to approve your
application, it must notify you in writing and must give its reasons. You
must also be told if the panel's recommendation was different from
the agency's proposal. You then have 40 days in England and Wales
to make representations to the agency OR request a review of the
agency's proposal by the IRM but *not to both* (see below for details of
the IRM). If you do not present your views, the agency can make its
decision. If you make representations to the agency decision maker
within 40 days in England and Wales, he or she may refer you back to
the panel.

If the case is presented again to the panel, the panel must give the
case fresh consideration. Alternatively, the agency may choose (but is
not obligated) to present the case to a different adoption panel (some
agencies have more than one panel, or may present cases to panels of
other agencies). The agency's decision after this second consideration
will then be final.

A final decision can also be made, after considering your views,
without the case going back to panel.

If you are still unhappy about the process, you may use the agency's
representation and complaints procedure.

How long does our "approval" last? Adoption Agencies Regulations
require that the approval should be reviewed at least annually until
a child is placed (at least every two years in Wales) or whenever the
agency considers a review to be necessary. Your agency should give
you clear information about this.

It is important that agency staff have regular contact with approved
adopters who are waiting to be matched with a child. Panels have a
useful role in reviewing the circumstances of waiting adopters and
sometimes receive regular, brief updating reports.

Summary of your rights throughout the approval process

- You must be shown a copy of the social worker's assessment section of the Prospective Adopter's Report (not including the medical information and references).

- You must be given an opportunity of at least five working days to comment on the assessment before it is presented to panel.

- You must be invited to attend the panel meeting.

- If the agency proposes not to approve your application, it must notify you in writing, and give its reasons.

- You must also be told if the panel's recommendation is different from the local authority's or agency's proposal.

- You have 40 days to present your views to the local authority or agency OR to apply to the IRM.

- If you contact the local authority or agency, it then decides whether or not to re-present the case to the panel. It may elect to present the information to a different panel.

- If the same panel considers the case, it must give it *fresh* consideration.

- If you request a review by the IRM, your case will be considered by an IRM panel, which will make a recommendation.

- The local authority or agency's decision after this second consideration will be final.

may have been identified before you began the adoption process (for example, foster carers adopting a foster child; birth relatives adopting a child; or applicants who apply to adopt a specific child).

An adoption agency can only match you with a child who has been "authorised" by the granting of a placement order or the giving of formal consent to placement for adoption by the child's parents (called a section 19 consent). However, if you are offering a FfA or concurrent planning placement, you will be caring for the child as a foster child till the authorisation is given.

Your social worker will visit you to discuss the details of a prospective child. If you express an interest in pursuing adoption of the child, the child's social worker and possibly the foster carer/s will also arrange to visit you. You must be given the Child's Permanence Report (CPR).

During these visits, it is important to discuss openly all relevant details about the child. Do not hesitate to ask questions because you fear it might seem "impolite" or "intrusive". After all, you are making a decision that will affect the child and you for the rest of your lives. If you decide not to proceed with a match for a child, you must return the Child's Permanence Report to the agency.

TERMS YOU NEED TO KNOW

The Child's Permanence Report (CPR) gives detailed information about the child, such as a physical description, his or her background, personality traits and currently known needs – educational, emotional, physical, health and development, etc. The social worker can provide valuable information and insight into the child's history, current relationships and behaviours. Social workers are required to provide the most up-to-date and complete information available.

Independent Review Mechanism (IRM)
Unit 4, Pavilion Business Park
Royds Hall Road
Wortley
Leeds LS12 6AJ
Tel: 0845 450 3956
Email: irm@irm.org.uk
www.independentreviewmechanism.org.uk

This is an independent review process, conducted by a panel. It applies to cases where an adoption agency in England is proposing not to approve, or to terminate the approval of, adoptive parents. If you receive notification in writing from your adoption agency that it proposes not to approve you, or to terminate your approval as an adoptive parent (this is called a "qualifying determination"), you can apply for a review EITHER to the agency (see above) OR to the IRM, but not to both.

If you decided to apply to the IRM, you must contact the IRM within 40 days of the written notification from the agency. The IRM will arrange for your case to be heard by an independent IRM panel, which you can attend.

The panel will make a recommendation which will go to your agency. The agency will then make the final decision.

Independent Review Mechanism Cymru
25 Windsor Place
Cardiff CF10 3BZ
Tel: 029 2034 2434
www.irmcymru.org.uk

This is available to people assessed by adoption agencies in Wales. It operates in a very similar way to the IRM in England.

HELPFUL PUBLICATIONS/WEBSITES

Resources listing children who are waiting to be adopted
The following publications and websites profile children who need families. If these publications feature a child you are interested in parenting, the child's social worker will still have to make sure that you are the right family for that child.

Link Maker/www.linkmaker.co.uk
A website that lists children needing new families and prospective adopters, throughout the UK. Prospective adopters can make their profiles available directly, or work with their agency in identifying possible matches. See Appendix 2 for details on contacting Link Maker.

Children Who Wait/www.adoptionuk.org
A listing of children needing new families throughout the UK, updated monthly and also available online. Available by becoming a member of Adoption UK. See Appendix 2 for details on contacting Adoption UK.

Adoption agencies also use **local or specialist media** to feature children needing adoption, e.g. *The Voice*, a weekly aimed at black communities, frequently features black children to attract the interest of black families. Occasionally, for example, during **National Adoption Week** in October (November in Scotland), television and national newspapers also alert the public to the needs of children needing adoption and may feature certain children.

The child's social worker should also discuss contact and support arrangements, the child's need for services after placement and adoption, for example, extra support in school, therapy, etc. There should also be discussion with you about the support that you are likely to need and about the services that the agency will provide, and proposed arrangements for contact (if any).

Adoption Support Services Regulations 2005 and accompanying Guidance place a duty on local authorities to assess the likely adoption support needs of a child when adoption becomes the plan and to make and agree an adoption support plan with prospective adopters when a potential match is being considered.

A proposed adoption support plan should be discussed with you before the match goes to panel and the proposals for adoption support should be included in the Adoption Placement Report. Once the match has been approved, you and the child's agency should finalise the arrangements for the support that the child and you are likely to need after placement and adoption. This could include, for example, financial support, the provision of therapy for the child, support groups or workshops for you, training for you to meet the child's needs, or respite care.

The medical adviser should provide a written health report on each child being considered for adoption. This report should include comments on birth history, family history, past medical history, current physical and mental health and behaviour and, if age appropriate, a developmental assessment. This report should assess the future implications for the child of their health history, and previous family and social situation, including their experiences in the care system.

Statutory guidance suggests that it is good practice for the medical adviser to meet before the matching panel with prospective adopters to share all appropriate health information and to discuss the needs of the child with whom you are matched. It is also good practice to provide a written report of this meeting.

THE ADOPTION REGISTER FOR ENGLAND AND WALES

The Adoption Register has two major elements:

- A computer database that stores details of children awaiting adoption where their own agency has not been able to find the right adoptive family, and details of approved adopters awaiting a placement where their own agency has not been able to match them with appropriate children; and

- A staff team of experienced database operators and family placement social workers who will look at the information to see whether they can suggest possible "matches" between children and prospective adopters. Since 2016, it has also been possible for prospective adopters to undertake their own search of the database.

Agencies refer to the Register those children who have been authorised to be placed for adoption but where there is not already a link identified locally which is being actively pursued. The children will be referred at the latest by three months after the agency has formally decided that a child should be placed for adoption and either:

- a placement order has been granted; or

- an application has been made for a placement order and all required consents, including that of the court, have been obtained; or

- the consent to placement for adoption has been obtained from parents with parental responsibility.

If you are a prospective adopter, you will be able to contact the Register direct on the helpline (see below). Once your identity has been checked, the Register will confirm that your details have been referred to them, give you information about the number of times your details have been sent out to social workers for consideration, and give you general advice. If your details have been sent out for consideration but a link is not being pursued, you can contact your social worker and ask about the reasons given by the child's social worker for not pursuing the link. You will also be able to search the database yourself.

Agencies can refer prospective adopters to the Adoption Register as soon as they have been approved by the agency and will usually do this if it seems unlikely that the adopters will be matched quickly with a suitable child in their own region. Agencies must refer prospective adopters (with their consent) to the Adoption Register three months after they have been approved if a match with an identified child is not being actively pursued. You can decide that you do not wish to give your consent to referral to the Adoption Register but this will, of course, reduce the opportunity for you to be matched with an appropriate child.

If your agency has not already sent your details to the Adoption Register, you will be able to contact the Register and complete a referral form. You must wait to do this until at least three months after the date on which your agency approved you as an adopter. The Register staff will then contact your agency and arrange your referral.

Matching children with adoptive families

Once your details have been recorded on the Register database, a search will identify child(ren) who match your approval profile. Relevant details of your family, including a written description (profile) and details of your approving agency will be sent to the child(ren)'s social worker who will consider the proposed link further. Information about your family can initially be sent up to five times to different workers for consideration. At this point your Register entry will be put "on hold" whilst the social workers are given time to pursue possible links with the children.

Adoption Register for England and Wales
Unit 4, Pavilion Business Park
Royds Hall Road, Wortley
Leeds LS12 6AJ
Adopter's helpline: 0345 222 9058
Email: mail@adoptionmatch.org.uk
www.adoptionregister.org.uk

To find out as much as you can about the prospective child:

- Talk to adults who know the child well.

- Discuss the Child's Permanence Report fully with social workers.

- Ask for a Child/Life Appreciation Day. This is a day when significant people in the child's life are invited to meet with the adopters to share information about the child. These people could include former foster carers, teachers, health visitors, child minders and former social workers. Family members may be involved too. Those involved will be able to share anecdotes and stories which may not be included in more formal reports.

- Meet significant family members and friends. The agency should have prepared you for the advantages of meeting the birth parent/s even if direct contact may not continue. Many adopters see this as important for the child's future.

- Have access to relevant sections of the child's file.

- Talk to foster carers about how they handle any difficulties.

- Consider the proposals for contact and whether you are comfortable with them.

- Receive and discuss a proposed written Adoption Support Plan.

Scotland's Adoption Register

Funded by the Scottish Government and launched in 2011, Scotland's Adoption Register and has two major functions:

- to provide facts and figures about adoption in Scotland;

- to add an effective Scotland-wide mechanism to existing arrangements for linking children and families for adoption.

7 John's Place
Edinburgh EH6 7EL
Tel: 0131 526 3240
Email: sar@adoptionregister.scot
www.scotlandsadoptionregister.org.uk

ARIS – Adoption Regional Information System Northern Ireland

ARIS operates on a similar basis to the Adoption Register.

Directorate of Social Care and Children
Health and Social Care Board
Level 3, 12–22 Linenhall Street
Belfast BT2 8BS
Tel: 028 9536 3098
www.online.hscni.net/aris

Link Maker

Link Maker is a social enterprise that provides an online service to help match waiting children with prospective foster carers and adopters. It aims to make placements faster and easier to find.

St Nicholas House
31–34 High Street
Bristol BS1 2AW
Tel: 0843 886 0040
www.linkmaker.co.uk

HELPFUL BOOKS

In Search of Belonging: Reflections by transracially adopted people,
Edited by Perlita Harris, BAAF, 2006
The first UK publication to give voice to transracially adopted children and adults. Brings together poetry, artwork, memoir, writing and oral testimony from over 50 transracial and transnational UK adoptees.

Considering ethnic origin, religion, culture and language when matching a child to a family

In general, it is in a child's best interest to be placed with parents who share as many aspects of their culture, ethnic background, language and religion as possible. Several studies have shown that these aspects of a child's background play an important role in developing a strong identity and in influencing the child's social adjustment as an adult. In Wales, the welfare checklist in section 1 of the Adoption and Children Act 2002 requires agencies to take into account, when making decisions about adoption, the child's religious persuasion, racial origin and cultural and linguistic background. However, in England the agency is expected to consider these issues alongside the other needs of a child and to be mindful of not causing detrimental delay. Instead, there is an expectation that families will seek to understand and support the child's identity needs.

HELPFUL BOOKS

Life Story Work: What it is and what it means by Shaila Shah and Hedi Argent, BAAF, 2006.
This is a guide for children that explains what life story work is, why it is important to do it, and how you can do it.

My Life and Me by Jean Camis, BAAF, 2001.
This is a book that you can use with the child as part of the life story work which may need to be undertaken.

Life Story Work (4th edition) by Tony Ryan and Rodger Walker, CoramBAAF, 2016.
This excellent guide provides insight, creative ideas and exercises you could use to do life story work in different settings.

Digital Life Story Work by Simon P Hammond and Neil J Cooper, BAAF, 2012.
A practical guide which looks at how to use computers, smartphones and camcorders with older children and adolescents in fun and creative life story work projects.

Child Appreciation Days by Andy Sayers and Roana Roach, BAAF, 2012
A guide which explores the benefits of child appreciation days for agencies, children and carers, and the practicalities of organising them.

Social workers, therefore, must give due consideration to these aspects when matching a child to a prospective family, but they must also consider the adoptive families which are available and the ability of those families to meet most of the child's needs. Guidance 4.7 states that 'A prospective adopter can be matched with a child with whom they do not share the same ethnicity, provided they can meet the child's other identified needs. The core issue is what qualities, experiences and attributes the prospective adopter can draw on and their level of understanding of the discrimination and racism the child may be confronted with when growing up.'

When considering placement of a child with a family from a different cultural background or ethnicity, social workers will want to be certain that the prospective adopters recognise that their own experiences may inhibit their complete understanding of, for example, racism that the child may encounter in the future. Social workers will also assess the prospective adopters' ability to help the child value, understand and experience various aspects of his or her own ethnicity and culture of origin, and to promote cultural continuity for that child.

Guidance 4.8 recognises that adopters will need flexible and creative support to be given by their agency. This could involve training sessions and providing opportunities for children to meet others from similar backgrounds and to practise their religion of origin.

A question of "competition"…?

Many prospective adopters are, understandably, irritated when they discover that several families may be considered, simultaneously, for one child. Adopters may feel upset that they have been placed "in competition" with other adopters in such a delicate matter. And, practically speaking, it seems a waste of resources – after all, aren't there hundreds of children waiting to be adopted?

However, it is important to remember that the child's welfare must always be the paramount consideration and that the key tasks are to find the adoptive family best able to meet the child's needs and to find them as quickly as possible. For these reasons, it may be necessary for several families to be considered at the same time before a decision is made about which one to concentrate on.

When considering more than one prospective adopter, social workers will consider issues of ethnicity, culture, religion, and language; the child's attachment issues, behavioural issues, personality, health, disabilities (if any), education, status in family (e.g. eldest/only), and physical characteristics (appearance); the child's wishes and birth parents' wishes; interests/hobbies/talents of child and adopters; contact requirements; and adopters' geographic location.

Although the child's agency may approach several adoptive families about a child, they must only present one adoptive family to the panel for a match with a child.

Do siblings have to be placed together?

In many cases, yes; in some, no. Children who are generally placed together include those who have a strong bond with each other and will benefit from staying together as a group.

In other cases, children may need particularly focused attention from the adopter/s, or may have other physical or emotional needs that are best met if the child is placed as an "only child". If a child suffers from extreme difficulties with attachment, placement as an only child may also be less stressful for the adoptive parent.

Sometimes large groups are split into twos and threes to allow families to more easily come forward to parent them. If a child is placed away from his or her siblings, it will be very important to consider arrangements for the children to have some contact with each other, if this meets the child's needs.

For more information about this topic, see:

- **Beyond Together or Apart? Planning for permanence for brothers and sisters** by Shelagh Beckett (CoramBAAF, 2018)
  A practice guide which highlights factors affecting decisions on placements of sibling groups.

- **Siblings in Late Permanent Placements** by Alan Rushton *et al,* BAAF, 2001
  A research study that explores the complexities of sibling placements and evaluates the outcomes in a sample of 1,330 children.

- **Adopting Large Sibling Groups** by Hilary Saunders and Julie Selwyn, BAAF, 2011
  A research study that considers what motivates adopters to take a large sibling group, examines the support available, the different agency practices, and the challenges and rewards.

6 The adoption panel considers the proposed match and makes a recommendation

You and the child will not be formally matched until the child has been authorised to be placed for adoption by the granting of a placement order or formal parental consent has been given.

Your social worker and the child's social worker and managers will meet to decide whether to support the match as being the right one for the child and for you. If they decide that it is, the social worker then completes an adoption placement report if you as prospective adopters agree that you want to go ahead. This report must be given to you at least ten days before the adoption panel considers the proposed match. You can comment on any of the content of the report. Adoption regulations set out what is required in this report.

Within the adoption placement report, the social worker must include:

- the agency's reasons for proposing the placement;

- your views about the proposed placement;

- your views about the proposed contact arrangements;

- the agency's proposals for adoption support services for the adoptive family;

- the agency's proposals for contact.

It will be the panel of the child's agency that will consider the match, which may or may not be the one which considered your approval. It will operate in a similar way and you will be invited to attend.

Legally, the adoption panel is required to undertake the considerations and recommendations with the child's welfare as the paramount consideration. Panel members will be aware that they must carefully balance the disadvantages of children remaining looked after by their local authority if the match is not approved, with the burden of ensuring that the applicants really can meet the needs of the child.

The panel will give its recommendation to approve or not approve the match to the agency, which will make the decision. It is unusual that matches are not agreed at this stage, although it can happen. There is no formal appeal process if a match is turned down. The panel may ask for additional information or work to be completed before they are ready to make a recommendation, rather than turn a match down.

7 You and the child are introduced

The child has been authorised to be placed for adoption. The match with the proposed child has been recommended by the adoption panel and approved by the agency – and by you. *Before* you meet the child, your social worker should give you the Adoption Placement Plan, setting out:

- the agency's reasons for proposing the placement;
- your views on the proposed placement and the agency's proposed contact arrangements;
- the local authority's proposal for adoption support services for the adoptive family;
- the agency's proposals for allowing contact by any person; and
- any other relevant information.

You should also take this opportunity to express any concerns or ask questions you may have. You and the agency will then agree a detailed introduction plan.

If the child is a baby, he or she may be placed with you after a fairly short intensive period of introductions. If the child is older, it will take longer and you will have a series of meetings with him or her before the child is placed. The purpose of these **introductions** is not only to meet the child, but also to help you and the child find out what living together will be like. You can do this by going through daily activities and routines, meeting friends and neighbours, looking at common interests, and focusing on the particular needs of the child. You may have had a one-off meeting before approval panel if the agency felt that this was appropriate for everyone to be sure the match was right. This is not offered by all agencies.

A child cannot be placed with you until you have notified the child's agency that you wish the placement to happen.

HELPFUL BOOKS

Me and my Family by Jean Maye, BAAF, 2011
A unique, interactive and fun "welcome to our family" book through which adopters can initially introduce themselves to the child, and for the child to work through and record the changes in their lives as they move to their new family. With space for drawings, writing and photographs.

What happens during the introductions?

During the introductions, you will normally first meet the child at his or her foster home. You will spend a few hours with the child, initially, and gradually spend more time on successive days. You can take this time to observe the child's interactions with the foster carer and to discuss the child's general behaviour and habits (eating, dressing, playing, likes/dislikes, etc).

After visiting the child in the foster home, the child will spend time at your house during the day and, eventually, may stay overnight and return to the foster home the next day. The length of time the introductory period takes depends entirely upon you and the child – older children may take longer to adjust to you (and you to them). You may also feel pressured by school term dates, holidays or other activities. But "speeding up" the process to meet these dates may not be in your or the child's best interests.

You can help the child adjust to the idea of moving in with you. Once you have been matched with the child, you will be asked to create a book for the child that tells about yourself and your family, and what it is like to live at your house. You can include photos of yourself, your home, family, neighbours, pets, and daily or favourite activities. It is helpful, especially for young children, to enable the child to "interact" with the book (by providing crayons or stickers with the book), thus making it his or her own (see *Helpful books* below).

Oh, the stress of it!

Spending time with the child at the foster carer's home can be a stressful experience for prospective adopters. You undoubtedly will be anxious to establish your own relationship with the child and you may find it difficult if the child is fairly attached to the foster carer. In addition, you may not agree with various ways in which the foster carer interacts with the child. It is important to remember, however, that these first visits are meant for you to observe the child so you can determine how best to meet his or her needs. Candid discussions with the foster carer(s) can give you valuable insight into the child that will help everyone in the long run. If you have any worries during this time, it is important for you to share them with your adoption social worker.

8 The child moves in (i.e. is placed with you)

In preparation for the child moving to your home, you will have a **final planning meeting** with your social worker, the child's social worker, foster carer/s, teachers – and anyone else significantly involved with the child – to discuss the placement date and to confirm details of the Adoption Placement Plan.

TERMS YOU MAY NEED TO KNOW...

Children's Guardian: a person appointed by the court to protect the child's interests during court proceedings for care orders and placement orders. This person might talk with the child to ensure there are no remaining issues that may affect the proposed match with the family. Because the child should not be matched with you until the placement order has been granted, the guardian will not need to visit you during care or placement order proceedings.

Curator *at litem* (in Scotland): has a role similar to that of the Children's Guardian.

Disruption: a term used to describe adoptions that do not work out. When a placement "disrupts", the child is returned to the care of the agency that originally placed him or her with you. A disruption meeting should be convened, followed by counselling or other support for the adoptive family (see also Section 5 of this Handbook).

Later-life letter: A letter written to the child, by a social worker, that explains (in children's terms) why the child was placed for adoption and how the placement occurred. The Adoption Placement Report should say when the later-life letter (and the child's life story book) will be provided (must be within 10 days of the adoption order).

Life story book: A "book" prepared with the child by a social worker, foster carer and/or adoptive parent that documents the child's life, from birth, through his or her life in foster care or residential care, to adoption. The information may include a description of the child's birth parent/s and/or birth family, other siblings or half-siblings, where that child was born, foster carers, and how the child came to be adopted. The purpose of the book is to provide a link for the child (when he or she is old enough to understand it) with his or her past and life history. The book is given to the adoptive parents who use the information sensitively, with the understanding that it belongs to the child. It must be provided to you within 10 days of the adoption order.

Reporting Officer: a social worker independent of the adoption agency who is appointed by the court to witness the birth parents' consent to their child's placement for adoption (section 19).

The Adoption Placement Plan

When an agency has decided on a placement it must provide 'as soon as possible' a *written adoption placement plan* to the prospective adopters.

Content of Adoption Placement Plan – Schedule 5, Adoption Agency Regulations 2005

HELPFUL RESOURCES

Contact in Adoption and Permanent Foster Care: Research, theory and practice edited by Elsbeth Neil and David Howe, BAAF, 2004.

Staying Connected: Managing contact arrangements in adoption edited by Hedi Argent, BAAF, 2002.

Contact after Adoption by Elsbeth Neil *et al*, BAAF, 2014

What is Contact? A guide for children by Hedi Argent, BAAF, 2004.

1   Whether the child is to be placed under a **placement order** or **consent of the parent/guardian**.

2   The arrangements for **preparing the child** and the prospective adopters for the placement.

3   The **date on which it is proposed to place the child** with the prospective adopters.

4   The arrangements for **review** of the placement.

5   **Whether the parental responsibility for the prospective adopters is to be restricted** and if so, the extent to which it is to be restricted.

6   **The support services** to be provided for the adoptive family.

7   **The agency's arrangements for allowing any person contact** with the child, the form of contact, the arrangements for supporting contact and the name and details of the person responsible for facilitating the contact arrangements (if applicable).

8   **The dates on which the child's life story book and later-life letter are to be provided** by the adoption agency to the prospective adopters.

9   Details of **any other arrangements** that need to be made.

10 **Contact details** for the child's social worker, the prospective adopters' social worker and out-of-hours contacts.

This final planning meeting will help everyone involved to understand each others' roles, responsibilities and expectations during the post-placement period. For example, you will want to know:

- the extent to which both social workers will be involved with the child during the placement;

- what contact (if any) the child will have with the birth family;

- if the child will have any continued contact with foster carers (research has shown that this can often be very important for children);

- what arrangements need to be made with other services (health, education) and who should arrange them; and

- what adoption support services are to be provided and when and how they are to be provided.

Settling-in grants

These are available for most children if they are needed. For details about these grants and about other financial support, see Section 2.

Contact

Research has shown that in many cases, adopted children can benefit from some form of contact with their birth parent and/or relatives. This can help a child have a sense of their history and heritage.

Contact after adoption may be planned if it is believed to be in the child's best interests. This may occur via "letterbox" or "indirect" contact, in which the adoptive parents agree to provide written information about the child and perhaps a photo, once every year. The letter is sent to the agency, from where it is then forwarded to the birth parent. The birth parent can provide information to the child in the same way. Some local authorities keep the photo on their files and invite a parent to view the photo in their office, where it is felt that there is less risk of a parent misusing a photo by placing it publicly on social media.

Contact may also occur directly, between the birth parent/s – and/or other members of the birth family – and child, by visits or meetings in public places (local restaurant, park, etc). It is important to remember that contact issues should always be decided with the child's interests in mind. Contact with siblings may be more informally arranged with their carers.

Where children have been authorised to be placed for adoption, or placed for adoption by an agency (including those under six weeks of age), contact is at the discretion of the local authority – there is not a duty to promote contact.

The child, local authority, parents, guardians, relatives (including siblings), holders of a previous contact order, child arrangements order or special guardianship order, can apply under section 26 of the Adoption and Children Act 2002 for a contact order. When the court makes a placement order it must consider actual or proposed contact arrangements, and the views of the parties, and may make a contact order even if there has been no application for one. Others, including the child's prospective adopters, can apply for section 26 contact orders with leave of the court.

Before making an adoption order the court has a duty to consider whether there should be arrangements for contact (orders or undertakings) and hear the views of all the parties. There is no "presumption" of contact. Contact orders can be made with adoption orders on application by parents and guardians, or others with leave of the court, or on the court's own initiative.

Birth family members or others seeking a section 51A contact order under the Adoption and Children Act 2002 after an adoption order has been granted, must first obtain leave of the court to apply.

Adoptive parents are *not* required to agree to contact, but may be advised to do so if social workers believe it will benefit the child. It is also important to remember that, as children grow up, they may seek to have contact with birth parents and relatives, and may search for them. See Section 4 for more information about resources for adopted people who are seeking contact with birth relatives.

When is the best time for the child to move?

There really is no "best" or "worst" time for placement. Generally, you will want to arrange moving in to suit the child. For school-age children, this means thinking about whether the child will need to change schools and when will be the best time to do this. For some children, moving in during school holidays may not be ideal, because there will be less structure and routine in the child's life, which he or she may find unsettling. You and the child will also have constant interaction during holiday periods, which may prove difficult for both of you at the start of a placement. For other children, this may be seen as a benefit.

The child generally benefits if your life continues "as normal" after moving in. "Celebrating" the event with large parties or exotic holidays will disrupt the child's normal routine and will make it harder for the child to adjust to the new family and surroundings. After all, returning from holiday or settling down after a party will entail another "change" for a child who has just experienced one of the most stressful changes in his or her young life.

You will need to arrange:

- an appointment with your GP and/or practice nurse to introduce the child and to discuss any questions you might have about the child's health records;

- visits with schools, nurseries or playgroups (if the child will have to change to a new one).

Your local authority must inform your GP and the education department of the child's placement with you. If the child is three years old or younger, your local health visitor should arrange to visit you. If this does not happen, contact your GP's surgery to make the appointment.

You may also wish to consult the GP or any consultants with whom your child was registered while he or she was in foster care. This can be arranged by your adoption social worker.

You should receive your child's health record book from your social worker. This lists your child's NHS number, immunisations, a growth record and other significant health information. If this record book is not available, ask your GP to provide a new one for your child. You will also have health information about the child in the Child's Permanence Report.

Having a child move in will almost be like giving birth. Do I have any legal basis for taking time off work?

Yes. Statutory adoption leave and statutory adoption pay (SAP) and also statutory paternity leave and statutory paternity pay (SPP) are now available. Since April 2016, this has also been extended to those taking children as a concurrent planning or FfA placement.

SAP and adoption leave are available to employees (male or female) adopting a child. They could be adopting on their own, or with their spouse or civil partner. Employers can offer additional pay or leave to the statutory requirement.

- SAP is paid at (currently) 90% of gross average weekly earnings for the first six weeks and £140.98 a week or 90% of average weekly earnings (whichever is lower) for the next 33 weeks.

- Adoption leave is available for 52 weeks but only the first 39 weeks are covered by SAP.

- To qualify for adoption leave the adopter must have completed 26 weeks continuous service with their employer by the end of the week in which they are notified of being matched with a child.

An adopter who wishes to receive SAP and take adoption leave will need to give their employer documentary evidence to confirm that they are adopting a child through an adoption agency. You will need a Matching Certificate, issued by your adoption agency, once you have been formally matched with a child.

Statutory paternity pay (SPP) and paternity leave are available to employees (male or female) who are the partner of someone adopting a child on their own or adopting a child with their spouse or civil partner.

- SPP and paternity leave can be taken for one or two whole weeks.

- SPP is paid at the lower rate of £140.98 (currently) or 90% of average weekly earnings (whichever is lower).

- To qualify for paternity leave the employee must have completed 26 weeks continuous service with their employer by the end of the week in which the adopter is notified of having been matched with a child.

An adopter (or their partner) who wishes to take SPP and paternity leave will need to give their employer evidence of their entitlement and will need information from the adoption agency for this. This is the Matching Certificate, described above.

If a couple is adopting a child jointly, the couple must choose who takes the SAP and adoption leave and who takes the SPP and paternity leave. If the person who was on adoption leave decides to go back to work early and forfeit the remaining leave and pay, the partner claiming paternity leave may be eligible for up to 26 weeks paid Additional Paternity leave.

SAP and adoption leave and SPP and paternity leave are not normally available to foster carers who adopt following a direct application to the court without the approval of the child's local authority or to step-parents who adopt a child – this is because these are not *agency* adoptions.

Employees who adopt a child from overseas (or whose partner does) may be eligible for SAP and adoption leave and SPP and paternity leave – the entitlements are the same as for those adopting a child in the UK. However, because of the differences in procedure for adoptions from overseas, the eligibility and evidential requirements are different:

- To qualify for either adoption or paternity leave employees must have 26 weeks' continuous service with their employer: that is, either 26 weeks ending with the week in which the adopter receives official notification or 26 weeks from the start of their employment.

- The information and evidence which employees must provide for paternity leave/SPP and adoption leave/SAP is written notification issued by the central authority that the adopter is eligible to adopt and has been assessed or approved as a suitable adoptive parent.

Both paternity and adoption leave can only start once the child has entered Great Britain.

It is important to keep your employer informed. You must notify your employer of your intention to take adoption leave or paternity leave within seven days of the date the adoption agency tells you that you have been matched with a child.

More information is available from:

- www.adoptionuk.org

- Guidance and current figures for pay is also available at www.gov.uk

- ACAS on 0300 123 1100 www.acas.org.uk

- There is a Statutory Payment Disputes Team on 0300 560630.

If you are ineligible for SAP because of low earnings, short length of service or self-employment, you could ask the child's local authority to consider making a payment of financial support equivalent to SAP under the Adoption Support Services Regulations 2005.

HELPFUL BOOKS

The Colours in Me: Writing and poetry by adopted children and young people edited by Perlita Harris, BAAF, 2008
A unique collection of poetry, prose and artwork by over 80 young contributors – ranging from 4–20 years of age – who reveal what it feels like and what it means to be adopted. Also available, a DVD containing readings from *The Colours in Me*.

Chosen: Living with adoption edited by Perlita Harris, BAAF, 2012
A collection of writings and poetry by over 50 adopted adults born between 1934 and 1984, which explore how they feel about adoption and what it has meant to them.

Proud Parents: Lesbian and gay fostering and adoption experiences by Nicola Hill, BAAF, 2013
A compelling collection of stories of lesbians and gay men who have adopted or fostered children, who share their experiences on the impact of adoption or fostering on their lives.

Could You be my Parent? Adoption and fostering stories edited by Leonie Sturge-Moore, BAAF, 2005
A collection of articles and interviews taken from BAAF's family-finding newspaper, *Be My Parent*, which create a fascinating snapshot of the process of adoption and foster care.

CoramBAAF's **Our Story series** provides an insight into the highs and lows of adoption through the real-life experiences of a wide range of families, including single parents, lesbian and gay couples, parents with birth children, those adopting from abroad, and many more. Visit www.corambaaf.org.uk/bookshop to see the series.

9. An adoption order is made through the court

HELPFUL GUIDE

Adoption: A guide for court users (Form A20), available from HM Courts and Tribunal Service.

The child's "legal" position

The child will not be your child, legally, until an adoption order is made by a court (see Section 2). You will have a "settling in" time, during which the social workers will visit you and the child at your home. You can apply for an adoption order at any time after the child has lived with you for ten weeks (if the child was placed with you by an agency). However, in agency placements you will share parental responsibility for the child from the time of placement.

The adoption certificate

Once the adoption is legalised by the courts, the child's adoption certificate is issued. This lists the adoptive family's surname and the date of the adoption order and the court where it was made. The child's actual birth certificate remains unchanged and can be accessed when the child is 18, or earlier if the child's birth name and the name of the birth mother are known. There is a short version of the adoption certificate which only lists the child's adoptive name and does not mention adoption. The certificate is available from the General Register Office for England and Wales or from the General Register Office for Scotland, or the Registrar General in Northern Ireland (see Appendix 2).

Can the birth parents oppose the making of the adoption order when the papers reach the court, even if the child has been placed with you for some time?

This is a complex question that depends upon the legal status of the child. If the parents have consented to the child's placement for adoption or have not withdrawn their consent, or the court has granted a placement order for the child, then the birth parents cannot oppose the making of the adoption order unless the court gives them permission to do so. For more information about this and about the court process, see Section 2 of this guide. However, courts do sometimes give agreement to parents to challenge the adoption order, and this can be stressful for prospective adopters. You should seek support and advice from the local authority in these situations.

Can we travel outside of the UK for a holiday with our child, if he or she has been placed with us, but the adoption has not yet been legalised in the courts?

Yes. If the adoption order has not yet been made, you must inform children's services of your intention to travel abroad. They will provide a letter giving you permission to take the child abroad. You must carry this letter with you, to avoid any difficulties with immigration officers who may question why you have a different surname from that of your child. If your child does not have a passport, you must have one issued in his or her birth name. You cannot take the child out of the UK for more than one month without the permission of the court or the permission of the birth parents with parental responsibilities.

10 Settling in and post-placement adoption support

As your child settles in to live with you and your family, you will continue to receive support from your social worker and from the child's social worker.

Statutory visits

The child's social worker (and possibly your social worker) will visit the child at your home within the first week. After that, they must visit at least once a week until the first review at four weeks to see how the child and you are settling in together. The social worker will arrange a statutory review within four weeks of the placement. Another review will follow three months after the first, and then six-monthly until the adoption order is granted. It is important to view these visits as a useful means of gathering support and information, rather than an intrusive invasion of your privacy. You and the child will gain the most benefit from these visits if you are candid with the social worker and raise the questions or issues that concern you.

What should I do if the child displays difficult behaviour during the social worker's visit?

Don't be afraid to treat your child "normally" – as you would if the social worker was not present. Most social workers have had many years' experience with children and will be well aware that the child may be very attention seeking or may find the social worker's visit unsettling. It will help your child if your response to him or her is consistent, no matter what the circumstances. They may need reassurance and reminders that they are going to be staying with you, especially if they have had a number of previous moves.

What do older children feel when being placed with a new family?

It is always helpful to try to put yourself in the child's shoes. How would you have felt, for example, at the age of four, upon moving in with a family of people you had met only a few weeks ago? The child may feel anxious, worried, perhaps somewhat frightened. He or she will need to understand the moving-in process in his or her "own" way. Social workers can help you and the child by giving the child as much information as possible in an "age-appropriate" way, explaining the purpose of the "introductions", and by providing information about you. Many foster carers also prepare the child for this event from the moment he or she arrives in their home.

You can also talk with your social worker about how best to minimise the child's anxiety, for example, by continuing contact with the foster family, the child's friends and activities, etc.

TERMS YOU MAY NEED TO KNOW...

Intermediary services – a service provided by adoption agencies on behalf of birth relatives. The agency sends a letter to the adoptive parents or adopted adults, informing them of the interest of a birth relative. Birth relatives are not provided with identifying information unless the adopted person agrees. This service is now offered by all adoption agencies following implementation of the Adoption and Children Act 2002.

Adoption Contact Register for England and Wales – a database of names and contact information of adopted people over 18 and their birth relatives. Either party can contact the Register. The Register enables both parties to declare an interest before either can act. In Scotland, this service is provided by **Birthlink**. (See Appendix 2.)

Support after the adoption

Parenting an adopted child is not always straightforward. Problems may crop up many months or years after the child is placed with you, especially at times of transition, e.g. change of school (see Section 4). You may have questions, from time to time, or you may need specific services and ongoing support to help you with the child. Whatever your needs, the adoption support provided by your local authority, adoption agency and other specialist post-adoption organisations can help you address issues you may face along the way. See Section 5 and Appendix 2 for more information.

In addition to support from your local authority, the following organisations provide post-adoption support.

- Adoption UK (www.adoptionuk.org)
- Post-adoption centres in different parts of the country
- Some voluntary adoption agencies

See Section 5 for contact details.

Adoption support services

Adoption Support Services Regulations 2005 and accompanying Guidance (there are equivalent regulations for Wales) place a duty on local authorities to assess the support needs of children and adopters with whom they are making placements and to decide what services will be offered, before the placement goes ahead.

Local authorities must appoint an Adoption Support Services Adviser (ASSA) who has responsibility for ensuring that people are directed towards appropriate services and that these are available. This will include a liaison role with health and education authorities and with local authorities and voluntary adoption agencies. Local authorities are required to publicise the identity and contact details of their ASSA.

The **Adoption Passport**, shown in Appendix 4, gives information about the kinds of post-adoption support that may be available and the statutory provisions that exist.

Social networking and contact

Social networking sites such as Facebook have had a huge impact on the way that people communicate with each other. Finding and contacting people is much easier than ever before, with both positive and negative outcomes.

it is important that you are aware of the way that the use of the internet, social networking and other technologies such as smartphones are changing the whole context of adoption contact. You need to know what you can do to protect privacy and security in the best interests of your child. However, you also need to recognise that there is a limit to how far you can control and monitor the use of these new forms of contact by your child and/or members of their birth family. You may need to manage complex situations which arise from unauthorised and unmediated contact.

HELPFUL BOOKS

Facing up to Facebook: A survival guide for adoptive families (second edition) Eileen Fursland, BAAF, 2013
Examines the way the internet, social networking and other technologies are changing the landscape of adoption contact, search and reunion. Provides essential information and advice.

Social Networking and You (second edition) Eileen Fursland, BAAF, 2013
A booklet for adopted young people on using social networking. Offers practical advice on sharing information (or not) and staying safe online.

Intercountry adoptions

Adopters may wish to adopt babies or toddlers from overseas, or they may have been moved by the plight of children abandoned in orphanages or affected by war or disasters in the countries they were born in. There are fewer countries that now allow or encourage intercountry adoption and the number of children placed in this way is small.

The Adoption and Children Act 2002 and the Adoptions with a Foreign Element Regulations 2005 provide for the regulation of intercountry adoption in England and Wales.

- Anyone wishing to adopt from overseas, including relatives, must be approved as adopters for intercountry adoption by a local authority or by a voluntary adoption agency registered to do this work.

- It is a criminal offence to bring a child who is not "habitually resident" in the UK to the UK for adoption without complying with these regulations.

HELPFUL GUIDES

Intercountry Adoption This introductory pamphlet sets out the basics about how to go about it, BAAF, 2010

There is information on adopting a child from overseas on the Government's website at: www.gov.uk/child-adoption/adopting-a-child-from-overseas

Information Pack for Intercountry Adoption, available from the Intercountry Adoption Centre. www.icacentre.org.uk

How do I apply to adopt from abroad?

You can obtain preliminary information about intercountry adoption from the Intercountry Adoption Centre or the Department for Education (DfE) adoption website (see Appendix 2 for contact details). The general process is then:

1 Contact your local authority children's services/social work department. It has a duty to provide, or to arrange to provide, a service for people wishing to be approved as intercountry adopters. It will supply general information and counselling about adoption. It will also discuss with you the children waiting for adoption in the UK. Some applicants may then choose to adopt in the UK; others will continue with intercountry adoption.

2 You must check the specific requirements of the overseas country of your choice. Some countries will not accept gay, lesbian or single adopters and some have rules about the maximum and minimum ages of prospective adopters. The DfE lists some countries as "designated" and others as "non-designated" for adoption. If you adopt from a "non-designated" country, you will have to "re-adopt" the child after you bring him or her to the UK. Your local authority will be involved in supervising the child's placement and will prepare a report for the UK court that will consider the adoption application. If you adopt from a "designated" country, you will have an adoption hearing in that country and will not have to re-adopt

the child once you return to the UK. There are also countries which, like the UK, have ratified the Hague Convention on intercountry adoption. You will not need to re-adopt here if you adopt under the Hague Convention. (These countries are listed on www.hcch.net/en/states/hcch-members)

3   Your local authority will arrange for a home study to be done or you can apply to one of the eight voluntary adoption agencies which are approved to assess the suitability of intercountry adoption and applicants. They all cover specific and limited geographical catchment areas. Applicants usually have to pay for this service. Charges vary among agencies but are currently often £6,000 or more. The home study will cover the same issues as for domestic adoption (see p. 19). The social worker will record details of the home study on the Prospective Adopter's Report. The Department for Education charges applicants in England and Wales a fee for its part of the process (see points 7, 8 and 10 below). This is currently £1,775. However, there is a means test and applicants wishing to adopt a close relative from overseas will be exempt. The overall cost of intercountry adoption is likely to be at least £20,000.

4   An adoption panel will consider your application and make a recommendation.

5   The agency decides whether or not to approve your application.

6   If your application is approved, it is sent, along with the Prospective Adopter's Report and the medical form, adoption panel minutes and other paperwork to the DfE or the National Assembly for Wales (the Central Authority).

7   The Central Authority will decide whether or not to issue a **Certificate of Approval**.

8   If you are approved, the Central Authority will send your papers to the authorities of the country from which you wish to adopt.

9   The agency in the child's country considers your application.

10 If the agency approves your application, your name is placed on a waiting list. When a child is identified, information about the child is sent to the Central Authority, which then sends it on to you. You should discuss this information with your agency's social worker, its medical adviser and/or your GP.

11 You travel to the child's country to meet the child. If you are married or civil registered, both of you must go to meet the child.

12 You must apply for UK immigration entry clearance for the child, and must fulfil the requirements of the child's country of origin (for example, completing paperwork and providing fees, if any).

HELPFUL ORGANISATIONS

Department for Education: Adoption website

www.gov.uk/child-adoption
Offers the latest news relating to the Department's processes for intercountry adoption; about the level of fees charged; and information on recent legislation changes affecting intercountry adoption, both in the UK as well as in particular countries.

Intercountry Adoption Centre

A confidential information and advice service for intercountry adopters at any stage of adoption or post-adoption. Services include an advice line; counselling for families or for young people who were adopted from overseas; training for professionals involved in adoption; and "consultation days" for prospective intercountry adopters.

22 Union Street
Barnet
Herts EN5 4HZ
Tel: 020 8447 4753
Email: info@icacentre.org.uk
www.icacentre.org.uk

Children and Families Across Borders (CFAB)

A voluntary organisation that helps families and individuals whose lives are split between different countries.

Victoria Charity Centre
11 Belgrave Road
London SW1V 1RB
Tel: 020 7735 8941
www.cfab.org.uk

In addition to the organisations listed here, there are organisations for families who have adopted from particular countries (for example, Children Adopted from China (CACH). Contact the Intercountry Adoption Centre for more information about these groups.

Adoption Support Fund

Local authorities can make applications to the Adoption Support Fund for funding to provide post-adoption therapeutic support, following assessment of the child's needs.

22 Station Road
Cambridge
CB1 2JD
www.adoptionsupportfund.co.uk

Will my adopted child automatically become a British citizen?

A child adopted outside the UK does not automatically receive British citizenship, even if both adoptive parents are British. The parents must apply for British citizenship for that child. A child adopted in the UK will become a British citizen if one of the adoptive parents is a British citizen. The exception to this is a child who is adopted by British citizens under Hague Convention procedures. He or she will receive British citizenship from the date of the adoption.

Health issues for children adopted from overseas

There may be very little medical information about a child adopted from overseas. It is important to be aware that the child may have an inherited condition that might not become obvious until he or she is older. You must also be aware that the child may have been exposed to infectious diseases, such as HIV, hepatitis B, hepatitis C, or tuberculosis, and that testing for these conditions may not be available in the child's own country. There is a high prevalence of pre-natal substance exposure in some countries. You must also be prepared for the possibility that the child has experienced severe abuse and neglect, and may suffer significant effects from this, even if he or she is very young. If the child has been in institutional care, this is likely to have impacted on their opportunity for good early attachments.

it is important that you are aware of these issues and are willing, and able, to address them once you have adopted the child. A CoramBAAF leaflet, *Children Adopted from Abroad: Key health and developmental issues*, is likely to be helpful. The medical adviser should be available to advise prospective adopters on health matters of children being considered for adoption from abroad, and ideally undertake a health assessment of the child.

Will we be entitled to the same adoption support as families who adopt in the UK?

Yes. Children adopted from another country may have a range of special emotional, developmental, health and educational needs, for which you may need specific services and/or post-adoption support (see Sections 4 and 5). However, you should keep in mind that your child's country of origin will usually want evidence that you can financially support the child, before agreeing a match, so you cannot expect to receive financial support to facilitate adoption of a child from overseas.

It will be important to address issues concerning your child's identity and self-esteem. You may find it helpful to seek support from groups and organisations associated with the child's birth country.

You are also able to receive financial support from the Adoption Support Fund (ASF) for therapeutic work that your child may need. This is applied for by the local authority where you live, after they have assessed your child's needs.

Legal and financial matters

In this section:

→ Gain a general understanding of the current laws and regulations concerning adoption and how they may affect you

→ Learn about your legal rights throughout the adoption process and afterwards, and about the rights of the child and the birth parents

→ Find out about the various costs involved with adoption and the financial assistance that may be available to some applicants

Introduction

Adopting a child is a legal process governed by rules and regulations designed to protect everyone involved in the process – most importantly the child, but also the adoptive parents and the birth parents. These laws are designed not only to protect you (and others), but also to help you safeguard your interests. Understanding your legal entitlements and obligations throughout the adoption process, therefore, can help you to be prepared and informed every step of the way.

Before we look at your legal entitlements and obligations throughout the adoption process, it helps to understand the laws that underpin these rights. The main laws in England and Wales are as follows:

- **The Adoption and Children Act 2002** is the statute governing adoption in England and Wales. The welfare of the child is paramount.

- **The Children Act 1989** made the welfare of the child paramount and includes basic principles, such as the definition of parental responsibility, and those followed by the courts in making decisions in children's cases; orders providing for the care and maintenance of children; and the responsibilities of local authorities for children. It is the major statute dealing with child care law and child protection law.

- **The Human Rights Act 1988** gives effect in the UK to rights and freedoms guaranteed under the European Convention on Human Rights.

- **The Protection of Children Act 1999** provides a cross-sector system for identifying people who are considered unsuitable to work with children.

- **The Care Standards Act 2000** governs the inspection and registration of fostering and adoption services. These functions are carried out by Ofsted.

The Adoption and Children Act 2002 was implemented at the end of December 2005. It changed significant parts of the adoption process, particularly in relation to planning for children. It is underpinned by Regulations, Guidance and National Minimum Standards. This chapter looks at legal and financial matters connected with adoption, in light of this new Act.

There are also many Regulations that govern the way in which adoption agencies carry out their functions (including the function of adoption panels); and those that prohibit agencies from approving adopters or foster carers who have been convicted or have been cautioned for "specified offences". The Adoption Support Services Regulations 2005, and the equivalent in Wales, detail the adoption support duties of local authorities.

HELPFUL BOOKS AND RESOURCES

- **Child Care Law: A summary of the law in England and Wales** by Deborah Cullen and Mary Lane, BAAF, 2014 (7th edition). A popular quick reference guide to the law relating to the care of children.

- **Child Care Law: Scotland** by Alexandra Plumtree, BAAF, 2014 (3rd edition). A popular quick reference guide to the law in Scotland relating to the care of children.

- **Child Care Law Northern Ireland** by Michael Long, CoramBAAF, 2018 (2nd edition). A quick reference guide to the law in Northern Ireland relating to the care of children.

- **Adoption Now: Law, regulations, guidance and standards** by Fergus Smith and Roy Stewart with Alexandra Conroy Harris, BAAF, 2013 (4th edition). A handy guide to all adoption legislation in England.

- **Adoption Order application**
  The application form for an Adoption Order can be printed from www.hmctsformfinder.justice.gov.uk/HMCTS/GetForm.do?court_forms_id=1082

- **Department for Education: adoption website**
  www.gov.uk/child-adoption

For written copies of legislation and explanatory notes about current legislation in the United Kingdom, contact:

- **Office of Public Sector Information (OPSI)**
  To read online and download, visit www.legislation.gov.uk

- **The Stationery Office**
  www.tsoshop.co.uk
  Tel: 0333 202 5077 (support line for online orders)

National Minimum Standards for Adoption

National Minimum Standards for Adoption were published by the Department for Education in 2011 (see Appendix 3). These standards are designed to improve the quality of adoption practice by informing *everyone* involved in adoption (including children, adopters, birth parents, local authority and voluntary adoption agencies) of what they can expect regarding issues such as timescales for placing children, matching children and families, the decision-making process, and access to services (including adoption support). The standards have the force of formal Guidance.

TERMS YOU MAY NEED TO KNOW

Accommodation/accommodated – England and Wales Under Section 20 of the Children Act 1989, the local authority is required to 'provide accommodation' for children in need in certain circumstances. The local authority does not acquire parental responsibility merely by accommodating a child and the arrangements for the child must normally be agreed with the parent(s), who, subject to certain circumstances, are entitled to remove the child from local authority accommodation at any time. They retain parental responsibility. A child who is accommodated is a looked after child.

Accommodation/accommodated – Scotland Under Section 25 of the Children (Scotland) Act 1995, the local authority must 'provide accommodation' for children in certain circumstances and may also do so in other situations. Normally, the accommodation is provided by agreement with the parent(s); they can then remove the child at any time in most circumstances. Parental responsibilities remain with the parent(s). A child accommodated under section 25 is a looked after child.

Adoption Order A court order that transfers sole parental responsibility to the adoptive parent/s. An adoption order usually cannot be made unless the child and adopters attend the adoption order hearing at court (unless there are special circumstances preventing the child or one of the adopters from attending). The court can make an order for contact along with the adoption order, although this is very rare.

If the court refuses the adoption order, the court may make another order under the Adoption and Children Act 2002 or the Children Act 1989 – including, for example, a special guardianship order, a child arrangements order, or revising of a placement order.

Brief Report – England A short report taken to an adoption panel when the agency decides early on that it has serious concerns about an adopter's application, but the applicant disagrees and wishes to proceed. The panel can either recommend that the application proceeds to full assessment, or that it is turned down. The recommendation is then accepted or not by the agency decision-maker. If he or she makes a qualifying determination that the applicant should be turned down, the applicant may apply to the Independent Review Mechanism (IRM).

Care Order A court order giving a local authority parental responsibility for a child which is shared with the child's birth parents, but enables the local authority to make the major decisions about a child's life, such as with whom and where the child should live, and consent to routine medical treatment.

Concurrent planning This is the term given to a small number of schemes currently operating. Children, usually babies or toddlers, for whom there is a chance that they might return home to their birth family, are placed with families who will foster them with this aim. However, the foster carers are also approved as adopters and will adopt the child, should the planned return home not be successful. In this way, the moves that a child may otherwise have to make are minimised. These schemes have to be run with the agreement and co-operation of the local court and to tight timescales.

Contact Order When a child is a subject of a placement order or section 19 consent to placement for adoption, there is no duty to provide contact but a contact order can be made under section 26 of the Adoption and Children Act 2002.

A section 8 contact order can be applied for or granted with an adoption order or after an adoption order is granted.

Emergency Protection Order A court order allowing the local authority, in an emergency, either to keep a child in a safe place (such as a hospital or foster home) or to remove a child (e.g. from a home) if it is considered the child is suffering, or is at risk of suffering, significant harm. The local authority must then apply to the court for a care order within the next seven days, if it is believed the child should remain in care to safeguard his or her welfare.

For both an emergency protection order and a care order to be granted by a court, the local authority must satisfy the court that the child is suffering, or is at risk of suffering, significant harm, attributable to an unsatisfactory standard of parental care.

Children's Guardian An officer from CAFCASS (Children and Family Court Advisory and Support Service) appointed by a court when:

i an application is made by a local authority for a care order or a supervision order for a child; or

ii when an application is made for a placement order or an adoption order that is opposed by birth parents.

A Children's Guardian may also be appointed in adoption proceedings in other circumstances, such as where there is a dispute about contact arrangements after adoption or the child does not wish to be adopted or is being adopted by relatives. The Children's Guardian is an experienced qualified social worker independent of the local authority.

The Children's Guardian conducts an independent investigation to establish whether or not the care order or placement order applied for is in the interests of the child. He or she meets with the child, the social worker/s and the birth parents. He or she is only likely to meet adopters if parents have been given leave to oppose the making of the adoption order, there is a dispute about contact after the adoption, or the child is being adopted by relatives. The Children's Guardian may also make other relevant investigations, if necessary. He or she then presents the findings to the court, which will then either grant or refuse the order applied for.

Fostering for Adoption (FfA) The Care Planning, Placement and Case Review and Fostering Services (Miscellaneous Amendments) Regulations 2013 (which came into force on 1 July 2013) allow an agency to give an approved adopter temporary approval as a foster carer for a named child. This enables a child to be placed as a foster child with carers without them having had a full fostering assessment or panel approval as foster carers. These will be children for whom the likelihood of eventual adoption is high. However, the child is fostered until, in most cases, work with birth parents and court involvement enables an adoption plan to be agreed and the child to be matched for adoption with these carers at panel.

Placement Order A court order which gives the local authority the legal entitlement to place a child for adoption. Parental responsibility is shared between the birth parents and the local authority and with the prospective adopters on placement.

Parental Responsibility This is the legal right to make decisions about a child. When a child is born to married parents, both have parental responsibility; if the parents are unmarried, the mother alone has parental responsibility but the father may acquire it by marrying the mother, by formal agreement with the mother or by a court order, or if they jointly register the birth with the mother. Others acquire parental responsibility by adoption – in which case the adoptive parents acquire all the responsibility formerly held by the parents; or by being appointed guardians – in which case they hold the full parental responsibility that a parent has; and in the case of a local authority:

- by the making of a care order, in which case the parent's or guardian's parental responsibility is shared with the local authority;

- or an emergency protection order, which gives the applicant parental responsibility subject to restrictions;

- or a placement order, in which case parental responsibility is shared with the local authority and can then be shared with the prospective adopters from the time of the placement.

Qualifying determination In relation to suitability to adopt a child – a determination made by an adoption agency that it considers a prospective adopter is not suitable to be an adoptive parent and does not propose to approve him/her as suitable to be an adoptive parent.

Reporting Officer An officer appointed by a court when a birth parent wishes to consent to the child's placement for adoption, or consent to an adoption order. The Reporting Officer ensures that the parent/s fully understand the legal effect of the consent and have given their consent unconditionally; the Reporting Officer then witnesses the birth parent/s' signed consent. After speaking with the Reporting Officer, if one or both of the birth parents decides not to consent to placement or adoption, the local authority will have to apply for a placement order or the adopters would have to ask the court to dispense with their consent to the making of the adoption order.

Child Arrangements Order A court order that determines with whom a child will live, and other arrangements, if separated parents cannot agree this. Child arrangements orders are sometimes granted to other relatives such as grandparents, or to foster carers. The making of a child arrangements order discharges a care order. The holder of a child arrangements order shares parental responsibility for the child with the child's parents.

Supervision Order A court order which places the child under the supervision of the local authority. The supervisor's duty is to "advise, assist and befriend" and the court may attach certain requirements to the order. A supervision order does not give the local authority parental responsibility.

Special Guardianship Order A special guardianship order – under section 14 of the Children Act 1989 – is a "halfway house" between a child arrangements order and an adoption order. The order gives parental responsibility to the special guardians, shared with the birth parents, but allows the special guardians to exercise parental responsibility to the exclusion of the birth parents on most issues (except adoption).

A special guardianship order discharges a care order. The special guardianship order comes to an end when the child is 18 years of age.

Special guardians cannot cause the child to be known under a new surname or be removed from the UK for more than three months without the leave of the court or written permission of each parent with parental responsibility.

Unlike adoption, the legal identity of the child does not change – they remain the child of their birth parents – and their nationality does not change. The birth parents remain liable for child support.

A special guardianship order is intended to be more permanent and legally secure than a child arrangements order but less so than the adoption order, and it will be harder for parents to discharge a special guardianship order than a child arrangements order – they would need permission of the court to apply, and it would only be granted if there had been a significant change in circumstances since the special guardianship order was granted and the welfare of the child required permissions to be given.

Summary of the legal entitlements and legal requirements of people involved in the adoption process

Everyone involved in the adoption process, including birth parents and adoptive parents, has legal entitlements throughout the process, but must also meet the legal requirements of legislation and regulations. These entitlements and requirements are listed in the table below:

THE CHILD

Legal requirements	• A child cannot be adopted once he or she has reached 18 years of age, or is married or civil registered. The application for the adoption order must be made before the child is 18.

	• Before a child can be placed with adoptive parents by an adoption agency, the child's circumstances must be considered, in compliance with regulations, by the agency. The agency must take into account the recommendations of the adoption panel (in relation to children whose parents consent to their adoption) and a decision must be reached about:
	  – whether the child should be placed for adoption
	  – whether a placement order should be applied for.

	• Children placed for adoption within the UK must be placed by an approved adoption agency, unless the placement is with a close relative. A close relative is the child's grandparent, aunt, uncle or sibling, whether of the full blood or half blood, by marriage or civil partnership.
	• The proposed match between the child and prospective adopters must also be approved by the agency, which will take into account the recommendations of the adoption panel.
	• The child's need for support services after placement and adoption must be assessed and a plan made before matching and placement, and contained within the Adoption Placement Report and Adoption Placement Plan.
Legal entitlements	• The welfare of the child is paramount for the court or agency making decisions about adoption.
	• The child's wishes and feelings about adoption decisions must be given full consideration, taking into account the child's age and ability to understand the issues. In Scotland, children must give written consent to adoption from the age of 12 years.

- All adoptions are registered in the **Adopted Children Register**. At age 18, the person adopted before 30 December 2005 may apply to the Registrar General to obtain a copy of his or her original birth certificate. This is available to adopted persons in Scotland at the age of 16. For people adopted *after* 30 December 2005, the route to disclosure of the original birth certificate and information about their adoption is via an adoption agency, not the Registrar General. If adopted before 12 November 1975, the adopted person must attend an interview with a counsellor before the birth certificate is made available.

- At the age of 18, the adopted person may apply to the Registrar General to be given the name(s) of registered birth relatives listed in the **Adoption Contact Register** wishing to have contact with the adopted person. It must be the adopted person who decides whether or not to contact the relative.

PROSPECTIVE ADOPTERS/ADOPTIVE PARENTS

Legal requirements

- The single adopter or at least one of a couple must be at least 21 years of age and domiciled in the UK or both the adopters must be habitually resident for at least one year in the British Islands.

- A birth parent adopting his child must be at least 18 years old.

- There is no legal upper age limit although adoption agencies need to consider age in relation to the needs of children.

- A person cannot be approved by an agency as an adopter if he/she has a conviction or caution for "specified offences" as described in Section 1 (*Who Can Adopt*) of this guide.

- Single people can adopt, and two people living together as a couple can adopt jointly whether or not they are married or civil registered couples.

- Unless they are a close relative, they must be assessed and approved by a UK adoption agency, after taking into account the recommendations of the adoption panel, as well as medical information and other checks regarding suitability (see Section 1 for detailed information).

- Must allow sufficient opportunities for agency social workers and others to visit their home after the child has been placed, to ensure the child's welfare. Those adopting through a local authority agency must also allow the agency to undertake statutory reviews of the placement.

- Those adopting children from overseas must comply with regulations for their approval and for notification of their local authority (see Section 1 for details).

- Prospective agency adopters have parental responsibility for the child placed with them which is shared with the local authority and the birth parents until an adoption order is granted. After the adoption order, only the adopters have parental responsibility.

Legal entitlements

- Prospective adopters are entitled to a fair and prompt service from adoption agencies, in accordance with the **Adoption National Minimum Standards** and **Statutory Adoption Guidance 2011 and 2013**

- Are entitled to comment and make representations about their assessment by the adoption agency.

- Are entitled to be assessed for support (including financial support) before and after placement and adoption.

- If the child has been made the subject of a care order or placement order for adoption, the birth parent/s of the child cannot remove the child from the adopters without the permission of the local authority holding the order or the leave of a court.

- If the child is placed with prospective adopters and they have filed their application for an adoption order in court, neither the birth parent/s nor the adoption agency can remove the child from the adopters' home without the adopters' permission or the permission of the court, whatever the child's legal status, unless there are child protection concerns.

- Prospective adopters can file their application for an adoption order after the child has lived with them for ten weeks.

- Once the court has granted the adoption order, the adoptive parents have sole parental responsibility for the child. Any previous court orders regarding the child are discharged although a section 8 contact order can be made with the adoption order (very rare).

- If prospective adopters do not wish to continue to care for the child placed with them, then before the child has been adopted they can ask for the child to be returned to the agency, which must receive the child.

BIRTH PARENTS

Legal requirements	• Birth fathers who are not married to the birth mother can acquire parental responsibility by agreement or by court order, by jointly registering the birth with the mother, by marrying the mother or by a parental responsibilities order.
	• Only birth parents who have parental responsibility for a child can give consent to the child's placement for adoption or ask the court for permission to oppose the making of the adoption order. If permission to oppose is granted, the court can dispense with the birth parents' consent.
	• Consent to the making of an adoption order must be given unconditionally and with full understanding. Evidence of that consent must be available to the court. Consent to placement cannot be given by a birth mother until the child is six weeks old. The birth mother's age is not a factor.
	• A birth mother cannot be compelled by law to disclose the identity of the birth father or her own family members, although she could be encouraged to provide information to help the child understand their history.
Legal entitlements	• Birth mothers acquire parental responsibility for their child automatically at the birth, as does a birth father married to the birth mother.
	• If a birth mother gives formal consent to her child's placement for adoption, she and a birth father with parental responsibility retain parental responsibility for the child. This entitles her/them to remove the child from the agency's foster care after seven days or from the adoptive placement after 14 days, unless the adopters have applied to the court for an adoption order or unless the agency applies for a placement order.
	• Once a child has been authorised to be placed by formal parental consent and/or the granting of a placement order, there is no duty to promote contact but the parents can apply for a section 26 contact order. Contact is at the discretion of the adoption agency unless a section 26 contact order is made.
	• All birth parents must be notified of any decisions made by the agency about their child. This includes:
	– that the child should be placed for adoption;
	– the placement of their child for adoption; and
	– that an adoption order has been applied for.

- Birth parents with parental responsibility are parties to the adoption proceedings and must be notified of the date and court venue of the hearings, and the court can hear their views. Increasingly, birth fathers without parental responsibility will be made parties to adoption and placement proceedings.

LOCAL AUTHORITY/ADOPTION AGENCY
(this information *does not* apply to step-parent or overseas adopters)

Legal requirements	• The agency must ascertain the wishes and feelings of the birth parents about the adoption and about the child's religious and cultural upbringing. The agency must place the child, as far as is practicable, according to these views, as well as taking account of the child's religious persuasion, racial origin and linguistic background.
	• If the whereabouts or identity of the birth father is known, the agency must try, if considered appropriate by the agency, to seek his views about the proposed adoption and offer him a counselling and information service, and ascertain if he intends to acquire parental responsibility for the child.
	• The agency must prepare, and agree with the adopters – before matching panel – an Adoption Placement Report, including contact and support proposals.
	• The agency must inform the local authority in whose area the child is placed, and the health authority, the education department and the adopter's GP when a child is placed.
	• The agency must visit the child in the adoptive home within one week of placement, and each week for the first four weeks. It must review the placement within four weeks of placement, again at three months after placement, and thereafter at six-monthly intervals until an adoption order is granted. The reviews must be chaired by an Independent Reviewing Officer (IRO).
	• When the application for an adoption order is filed with the court, the agency must prepare a court report (known as an Annex A report) concerning the background of the child and birth family, and the adopters, the child's welfare in placement for adoption, the reasons for the agency's decision making, and the agency's opinion as to whether the order applied for is in the child's best interests.
Legal entitlements	• The local authority has parental responsibility for a child who is the subject of formal consent to placement for adoption, and adopters will share parental responsibility with the agency and birth parents from placement.

- If the local authority holds a placement order or formal consent to placement for the child, it shares parental responsibility with the child's birth parents, but has the power to make major decisions about the child (such as where the child lives and with whom), even if this is against the birth parents' wishes, and make decisions about contact until and unless section 26 contact orders are made.

- The local authority holding a placement order or formal consent to placement is a party to the application for an adoption order and can have its views heard by the court on that application.

The role of the courts in the adoption process

The role of the courts throughout the process of adoption is to ensure that the welfare of the child is paramount and that the legal rights of all parties involved in the process (especially the child's rights) are protected.

Three different courts can undertake adoption proceedings:

- Magistrates Court (known as the Family Proceedings Court)
- County Court Adoption Centre
- High Court

What is the general process for applying for an adoption order?

To apply for an adoption order, you must file an application with the court. If a court has previously made orders involving the child (such as a care order or placement order), then the application for an adoption order should be filed in that same court. The application can subsequently be transferred to another court, e.g. closer to your home area or a County Court Adoption Centre.

You may not require legal advice or representation to file the application if:

- the birth parents have consented to the child's placement for adoption and not withdrawn that consent;

  AND

- given consent to the making of an adoption order;
- the parents have not been given leave of court to oppose the adoption order.

HELPFUL GUIDE

Adoption: A guide for court users (Form A20)
Available from HM Courts and Tribunal Service.

Usually staff from your adoption agency will assist you with making the application and providing some of the accompanying documents.

You will almost certainly require legal advice and assistance if the birth parents have been given leave to oppose the adoption order and/or have applied for a child arrangements order to be made with the adoption order. It is vital to consult a solicitor who has experience in adoption law.

If the child is looked after by the local authority, then it should pay your legal costs. If you are on a very low income, you may be eligible for public funding to pay legal costs; your solicitor will advise about this.

If you do not wish your identity to be disclosed to the birth family, you can ask the court for a serial number that replaces your name and address on the application and court documents.

The following documents must be filed at the court, along with your application. The application must be filed in triplicate on a standard court form. If the application is opposed by the birth parents, you must also file a "statement of facts" in triplicate (see below).

- your marriage or civil registration certificate (unless you are a single adopter)*

- a decree absolute, if you have been divorced, or dissolution of civil registration certificate*

- a copy sealed by the court of the placement order or the section 19 parental consent that the child is subject to

- if you are non-agency adopters (usually in step-parent and intercountry adoptions), any documents available to you that show the birth parent/s have consented to the adoption

- your adoption agency (or local authority, for step-parent or intercountry adoptions) will file an Annex A report at the court when the court notifies the agency of your application.

There is a court fee for the application. Currently, the fee is £30 per child in the Magistrates Court and £170 per child or sibling group in the County Court and High Court. If the child has been placed for adoption by an adoption agency, which is supporting the application, the agency is

---

*These must not be photocopies.

expected to pay the court fee (Adoption Support Services Regulations) if it supports the adoption.

If the birth parents consent to the application for an adoption order, the court will appoint a Reporting Officer. This person interviews the birth parents, ensures that they give their consent unconditionally and with full understanding, and if so, witnesses their written consent.

Speeding up the court process in adoption

The DfE has been working with the Department for Constitutional Affairs (which is responsible for courts in England and Wales) to speed up the legal process of adoption. This is being achieved with several initiatives, including: increasing the number of judges dealing with family work; making better use of judges and magistrates with expertise in adoption; finding new ways to manage adoption cases and thus reduce delay; and improving communication between everyone involved in the court adoption process.

Adoption Centres have been established in England and Wales to centralise all adoption work from county courts. The centres have specialist judiciary and staff who are experienced in adoption proceedings. If you have made an application to a County Court that is not an Adoption Centre, the application will be transferred by the court.

Section 1 of the Adoption and Children Act 2002 requires the court to timetable adoption proceedings quickly, because delay is likely to be prejudicial to the child's welfare.

What happens if the birth parent/s are given leave to oppose the adoption?

If the birth parents oppose the application:

- You are required to ask the court (via your solicitor if you have one) to dispense with the birth parents' consent. This is done by filing with your application a "statement of facts" (in triplicate) setting out the child's past and current circumstances and the reasons why you believe the legal grounds for dispensing with parental consent are met. The statement of facts should be prepared by your solicitor or by the Legal Department of the local authority if the child is in care. Legal grounds for dispensing with consent must be proved to the court. The grounds (section 52 Adoption and Children Act 2002) are:
    - the parents cannot be found; or
    - the parents are incapable of giving consent; or
    - the welfare of the child requires the consent to be dispensed with.

- If a parent is given leave of court to oppose the adoption order, the court will appoint a **Children's Guardian** to examine all aspects of the adoption order application and to prepare a report advising the court as to whether the adoption order is in the best interests of the child, or whether some other order might be better. The Guardian will interview you, the birth parent/s, the social workers and, probably, the child. The Guardian will also undertake any other investigation considered necessary or ordered by the court.

When must adopters attend court proceedings and why?

There are two types of court hearings: "directions hearings" and the final hearing for the adoption order application. You would not usually be required to attend directions hearings, as this is when the court will determine whether there is any challenge being made by the parents. You are not always required to attend the final hearing. You should bear in mind that birth parents will also be entitled to attend the hearings and you may need to consider with your solicitor and agency what precautions may need to be taken to avoid meeting them. The court can decide that you and your child should attend at a later date – usually 21 days after the order is made, to allow time for challenge if the birth parents might challenge the order and you want your identity to be kept confidential.

Directions hearings There may be several brief court hearings before the final hearing at which the application for the adoption order is decided. These directions hearings enable the court to advise you and/or your solicitor (and other parties) about procedural and evidential matters that need to be resolved; for example, the appointment of a Children's Guardian; the date by which the adoption agency must submit the Annex A report; and a mutually convenient date for all parties and witnesses to attend the final hearing.

Final hearing Although you are required to attend this hearing because you are the applicant/s, the court may decide to hear an application in your absence. You will be represented in court by your solicitor. The judge or magistrates may want to see you in person. If the application is opposed, the judge or magistrates will also want to see the birth parents. The judge or magistrate will hear oral evidence and then consider all the circumstances of the case (including the content of the Annex A and Guardian's report) and will decide if the adoption order is in the best interests of the child.

Adoption visit If the court decides that you and the child do not need to attend the final hearing, the judge can arrange an "adoption visit", which is an informal celebration when you and your child can meet the judge so he or she can confirm the adoption order has been made.

Other parties

Local authority If the child is subject to a placement order or section 19 consent, or the local authority has prepared a report in a non-agency adoption (step-parents or relatives), the local authority is a party to the adoption order proceedings. The local authority solicitor and at least the child's social worker (also sometimes a manager or other social work witness) will attend court and participate in the hearing – presenting to the judge the local authority's views on your application.

Birth parents Those with parental responsibility will automatically be parties to the proceedings. Sometimes the court will make a father without parental responsibility a party, and he is then entitled to legal representation in court.

The child Sometimes the court makes a child a party to the proceedings so that he or she can be legally represented. The child's solicitor will usually be instructed by the Children's Guardian. Unless the guardian has asked the court to excuse the child's attendance, he or she will be required to attend court, but only if the judge has decided that adoption is in the child's best interests and so that the adoption order can be made with the child present. Therefore, the child is not required to attend court to hear the evidence or the legal arguments for and against your application.

Where your identity is not known to the birth parent/s, and if you and the birth parent/s are both attending the final hearing (or any directions hearing), your solicitor should ensure that arrangements are made by the court so that you arrive at separate times and do not appear in the courtroom at the same time.

At what age will my child be permitted to read his or her children's services records?

Your child may be able to read information held about him or her, or any records, depending on the child's age and level of understanding if this is assessed to be needed as part of the adoption support plan. Adoption agencies are generally moving towards a more open approach and current practice is certainly to share information as needed. Each case is determined on an individual basis. Your child will not have access to information held about any third party involved. When your child is 18, he or she will be able to access information held about themselves by the agency and the court and is entitled to receive their Child Permanence Report (CPR).

NMS 2.1 requires that:

The adoption agency is active in its efforts to obtain for the child clear and appropriate information from the birth parents and birth family about:

- themselves and the child's birth and early life;
- why the child could not remain with their birth parents;
- why the child was placed for adoption;
- health issues of the birth parents and their children;
- the views of the birth parents and birth family about the adoption and contact; and

- up-to-date information about themselves and their situation.

Local authorities must specify in the Adoption Placement Plan before the placement the dates on which the later-life letter and the child's life story book will be given to you. This should be within 10 working days of the adoption hearing.

What information can we and should we have?

You should have been given a copy of your PAR but are not entitled to see information provided by your referees unless they consent to disclosure. The agency must also make accessible to you information about your adopted child.

Statutory Adoption Guidance 4.24 states that, when considering a match between prospective adopters and a child:

> It is unacceptable for agencies to withhold information about a child and provide a picture that bears little relation to the reality. The information provided must include full details of the child's background. This includes the history of any abuse or neglect and/or sexualised behaviour on the part of the child, their history in care, including the number and duration of placements, education and progress (or difficulties), behaviour and comprehensive information about physical and mental health and development and the implications for the future.

What is the legal position if I/we decide that we no longer wish to care for a child placed with us by an agency for adoption? Can I/we return the child to the agency?

If you are prospective adopters and the child is living with you *before* an adoption order is made, you have parental responsibility for him or her shared with the local authority and birth parents. You can ask to return the child to the agency, which is obliged to receive the child. If the child leaves, you will no longer have parental responsibility.

Once an adoption order is granted, you, as adoptive parents, become the child's legal parents, and have sole parental responsibility for the child, until and unless a subsequent adoption order is granted to other people.

The legal status of an adopted child is the same as a child living with birth parents – the adopted child is regarded in law as is they had been born to the adopters. Once adopted, the child cannot be "returned to the adoption agency", and the adoption agency is not obliged to receive the child into its care. However, you can ask the local authority where you live to accommodate the child – he or she will then become "looked after". However, the local authority will explore with you what help could be offered to you and your child to try and enable the child to remain in your family.

Like any family, you can ask the local authority children's services department to assist and advise you in caring for the child, and if you feel you cannot cope with the child at home, you can ask for the child to be accommodated by the local authority. The decision as to whether accommodation is in the best interests of the child rests with the local authority. That accommodation will be in foster care or a children's home for as long as is considered necessary. Like any parents, you will be asked to participate in decision-making about your accommodated child, and you may ask for his or her return.

However, if the local authority considers the child to be at risk of significant harm, attributable to the standard of your parental care, or that the child is beyond your parental control, it may institute court proceedings for an emergency protection order or care order, as with any family. As parents, you will be entitled to legal aid automatically.

Money matters

How much does it cost to get an adoption order?

Court fees: This is currently £170 in the Family Court.

If the child is being adopted from local authority care and the local authority supports the application, the expectation is that it will pay the court fee if it supports the adoption.

Legal costs: If the birth parent/s oppose the adoption, the local authority will attend the court – adopters will not usually be invited. If the local authority supports the adoption, they will usually send a lawyer to represent the joint position.

Other costs: Adoption agencies can and usually do charge a fee for an assessment or prospective adopters of children from overseas. If you are adopting from overseas, you will also incur travel expenses and may have to pay additional fees to authorities in the child's country of origin (see Section 1 for more details) and fees to the DfE and the local authority for writing a report for the country of origin.

What types of financial assistance may be available to help with our adopted child?

For children adopted from care, financial help may be available during placement of the child and before the adoption order is granted.

Different types of financial support may be available to prospective adoptive parents. This support is based upon the financial need and resources of the adoptive family and upon the particular costs the family will incur as a result of being introduced to the child, and the child going

HELPFUL ORGANISATIONS

Children and Family Courts Advisory and Support Service (CAFCASS)
Practitioners who provide advice to courts about the welfare of children. CAFCASS administers the children's guardians service.

National Office
3rd Floor, 21 Bloomsbury Street
London WC1B 3HF
Tel: 0300 456 4000
Email: webenquiries@cafcass.gsi.gov.uk
www.cafcass.gov.uk

Child Law Advice Line
0300 330 5480

Community Legal Service
A government initiative designed to ensure that everyone has access to quality legal advice and information, including by funding legal costs for those on a very low income without significant capital. The service can be provided by Citizens Advice Bureaux (CABs), solicitors' firms and legal advice centres that have been awarded the Community Legal Service Quality mark.

You can find the *Community Legal Service Directory* at your local library. It lists all the law firms and advice centres which have the Quality Mark, and indicates whether firms offer free advice or if they charge.

Tel: 0845 345 4345 for advice and information about CLS providers or about the CLS directory.
www.legalservices.gov.uk

Coram Children's Legal Centre
Specialises in law and policy affecting children and young people. Produces information sheets and booklets. In addition to policy and campaign work, CLC also provides an advice and information service (free and confidential legal advice).

Tel: 01206 714650
www.childrenslegalcentre.com

Family Rights Group
A national organisation that advises families who are in contact with children's services, about the care of their children.

The Print House
18 Ashwin Street
London E8 3DL
Tel: 020 7923 2628
Advice line: 0808 801 0366
Email: office@frg.org.uk
www.frg.org.uk

www.family-solicitors.co.uk
An online information service that provides advice and specific information about adoption, and lists solicitors who specialise in adoption and other aspects of family law.

www.compactlaw.co.uk
An online legal and information service that provides specific information about adoption law.

to live with them. Each local authority will assess the family's need in order to determine if support is necessary. The types of support *may* include:

* travel expenses for introductions to the child;
* travel expenses for the child's contact with his or her birth family;
* costs of beds, wardrobes, etc (for example, if you are adopting a sibling group);

- special equipment and house adaptations;

- payment for loss or damage;

- ongoing financial support, which may be paid before an adoption order. This is likely to be paid less child benefit and tax credits and should normally not exceed what would be paid to foster carers of the child; it may be used to support prospective adopters who are not entitled to statutory adoption pay (SAP), e.g. if they are self-employed;

- other financial support that might include respite care, emergency support, domestic help, therapy for the child, or other costs involved during the placement.

If the child is less than five years old, placed singly and without significant special needs or disabilities, it is unlikely that most of these expenses will be met by local authorities or that ongoing financial support will be paid.

State benefits for a child's special needs (such a Disability Living Allowance or Carer's Allowance) may be available to adopters from placement. Child benefit is payable from the date of placement for adoption, and tax credits can be claimed.

TERMS YOU MAY NEED TO KNOW

Fostering allowance – financial support payable by local authorities to foster carers (but not to prospective adopters), including those offering FfA or concurrent planning placements. There are nationally recommended rates for foster carers but these do vary considerably between local authorities.

Settling-in financial support – most local authorities will make available a settling-in grant. This is a discretionary grant and you can ask your social worker how to apply for it.

Is financial support available after an adoption order?

Adoption allowance

Financial support can be paid to adoptive parents before and after the adoption order is granted. This allowance is permitted under the Adoption Support Services (Local Authorities) Regulations 2005 (and equivalent regulations in Wales). Financial support is designed to facilitate adoptions of children who might otherwise not be adopted, due to the financial cost to the adopters. The allowance is not taken into account for income-related benefits and income tax and may be paid on a weekly or monthly basis, or as a one-off payment.

According to the Adoption Support Services Regulations 2005, financial support may be paid if one or more of the following circumstances exist:

- the child has not been placed with the adoptive parents for adoption, and financial support is necessary to ensure that the adoptive parents can look after the child if placed with them;

- the child has been placed with the adoptive parents for adoption, and financial support is necessary to ensure that the adoptive parents can continue to look after the child;

- the child has been adopted, and financial support is necessary to ensure that the adoptive parents can continue to look after the child;

- the local authority is satisfied that the child has established a strong and important relationship with the adoptive parent before the adoption order is made;

- it is desirable that the child be placed with the same adoptive parents as his or her brother or sister (whether of the full blood or half blood) or with a child with whom he or she has previously shared a home;

- the child needs special care which requires a greater expenditure of resources by reason of illness, disability, emotional or behavioural difficulties or the continuing consequences of past abuse or neglect;

- on account of the age, sex or ethnic origin of the child it is necessary for the local authority to make special arrangements to facilitate the placement of the child for adoption.

The amount payable as financial support is determined by the local authority, which takes into account the adopters' financial resources and commitments (not including the value of their home).

Financial support paid after adoption must not include any element of fee or reward which the carers were receiving as foster carers of the child. However, the exception to this is when foster carers wish to adopt a child whom they are fostering. They may continue to receive financial support, which includes a reward element for two years and, in some situations, for longer, after an adoption order.

Adopters receiving regular financial support must inform the local authority of changes in their financial or other circumstances and supply an annual statement of their finances. Financial support must be reviewed annually.

Payment of financial support will not affect other benefits you receive, such as Income Support, except the element for the child. Contact your benefits provider for more information.

Can I apply for financial support after an adoption order?

Yes. The Adoption Support Services Regulations 2005 provide that adoptive families can ask for their need for adoption support, including financial support, to be assessed at any point before or after the adoption order until their child is 18 and ceases full-time education or training. Local authorities have a duty to do an assessment if asked. You would need to apply to the local authority that placed the child with you unless it is more than three years since the adoption order. If this is the case, you need to apply to the local authority where you live. However, if you were receiving regular financial support before the adoption order and continue to receive it, the responsibility for that financial support continues with the placing agency, wherever you live.

Your entitlements regarding financial support

There is no national rate for paying financial support and this is determined by each local authority as part of the assessment process.

However, local authorities are *required* to:

- *consider* if financial support should be paid;

- inform adopters about available financial support;

- give adopters written notice of the proposed decision about financial support;

- hear representation from adopters about financial support if they don't agree with what the local authority is proposing;

- review the financial support annually.

If you believe your needs have not been fairly assessed or if you have other complaints about the adoption support, use your local authority complaints procedure in the first instance. If you still are not satisfied, you may contact your Local Authority Ombudsman.

The placing local authority has responsibility for adoption support for three years from the making of the adoption order. After this, responsibility moves to the local authority where the adoptive family lives. However, as Adoption Guidance 9.20 states:

> *The placing local authority is responsible for the continued payment of financial support agreed before the adoption order is made. It is important that this provision is not misinterpreted as justification for a decision to pay ongoing financial support for a period limited to three years from the making of the adoption order. Any decision on the provision of support must be based on the needs and resources of the child and family. This applies equally to a decision about the period for which financial support is payable.*

Other benefits

The local authority cannot duplicate the financial help you might receive from state benefits (and tax credits). Other types of benefits may be payable to adoptive parents by the Benefits Agency, as for any child in their family, under certain circumstances. These benefits are not automatically payable if you have an adopted child with physical, mental or emotional difficulties. However, it is worth knowing which benefits exist and are available in case you require financial support at some point in the life of your adopted child. You will need to find out which are means tested. These benefits currently include:

- **Carer's Allowance** Adoptive parents, like all parents of children with disabilities, may be eligible for Carer's Allowance *in addition* to Disability Living Allowance, as long as one parent is not in full-time employment or earning more than £50 per week (irrespective of the partner's income). Many adoptive parents (usually mothers) are unable to take jobs because the needs of their children are so immense and because childcare arrangements are generally unable to meet the children's specific needs.

HELPFUL RESOURCES

For information about benefits, contact:

- your local post office (applications and information about various available benefits);

- your local Citizens Advice Bureau (offers advice and information) – check your local phone book for the Bureau nearest you;

- your local authority's welfare rights department (usually located within social services);

- *Community Care* magazine – www.communitycare.co.uk – has articles on the benefits system.

Am I entitled to leave during the adoption of my child?

Yes – both statutory and adoption leave and pay and also statutory paternity leave and pay are now available (see Section 1).

Benefits provisions of the Carers and Disabled Children Act 2000

If your child has a physical or mental disability as defined by this Act, then you or your child may be eligible for:

- direct payments to 16- and 17-year-old young people who have a disability;

- direct payments to carers to meet their own assessed needs – this may mean that parents of a disabled child could receive a direct payment, rather than use the services provided by the local council, perhaps because they think existing services are not suitable or appropriate for their child.

Contact your local Benefits Agency for more information about these benefits and see Section 4.

Schooling and education

In this section

→ gain a general overview of the types of problems some adopted children may have in school

→ learn how schools can meet the needs of children who have difficulties

→ understand the process of obtaining special educational provision for your child

→ find out about current government initiatives and regulations to help you understand what support and services your child may be entitled to at school

→ find organisations and resources that can help you support your child at school and help you obtain the services that meet his or her specific needs

Introduction

Going to school is one of the main activities of childhood. Schooling not only teaches children academic skills, but also provides essential lessons in identity formation, relationship building and socialisation. Many adopted and fostered children have **learning difficulties** that may affect their ability to learn and/or their ability to socialise successfully with other children. According to the Department for Education, 'learning difficulty' means that '... the child has significantly greater difficulty in learning than most children of the same age; or the child has a disability that prevents or hinders him or her from making use of the kind of facilities generally provided for others of the same age in mainstream school or mainstream post-16 institutions.

In some cases, children may be identified as having social, emotional or mental health difficulties. The SEN (Special Educational Needs) Code of Practice states that schools should have clear processes to support children and young people, including managing any disruptive behaviour so it does not adversely affect other pupils.

Some children may not be officially "identified" as having either of these difficulties, but may nevertheless have problems with academic and/or social skills at school.

It is important that adoptive parents recognise the possibility that their children may have difficulty at school. Your child will benefit if you are observant of his or her schoolwork and behaviour, and communicate openly with school staff. At the same time, it is also important to try to keep a "balanced" view of "normal" childhood behaviours and social interactions at school.

All children who have been looked after or who are adopted are recognised as being "disadvantaged" and so are eligible for the **Pupil Premium** grant.

Adopters should be aware that, over the life of this handbook, there may be significant changes in the provision of education services and the organisation of schools and therefore in some of the information given in this chapter. Up-to-date information is available from the DfE website at www.education.gov.uk, or from your local authority.

What are we entitled to know about our child's educational history?

The Children Act 1989 requires local authorities to provide a **Care Plan** for every child in its care. The Care Plan should '...take account of the

HELPFUL BOOKS

... to inform educational and social work professionals about the impact of emotional trauma on a child's ability to learn:

Attachment, Developmental Trauma and Executive Functioning Difficulties in the School Setting by Marion Allen, Family Futures, 2008
Provides strategies and interventions to manage behaviour and establish an environment which will enable children to achieve their personal and academic potential.

Inside I'm Hurting: Practical strategies for supporting children with attachment difficulties in schools by Louise Michelle Bombèr, Worth Publishing, 2007
Provides educational professionals with a much-needed classroom handbook of strategies, practical tools and the confidence for supporting children (who have experienced trauma) from an attachment perspective.

Learn the Child: Helping looked after children to learn (second edition) by Kate Cairns and Chris Stanway, BAAF, 2013
Good practice guide on helping and supporting traumatised children and young people in their learning.

Supporting Children in Public Care in Schools: A resource for trainers of teachers, carers and social workers by John Holland and Catherine Randerson, Jessica Kingsley Publishers, 2005
A comprehensive training resource which provides guidance on how to support children who have faced loss as a result of significant changes in placement.

child's educational history, the need to achieve continuity, and the need to identify any educational need which the child may have, or carry out any assessment in respect of any special educational need'. Within the Care Plan, local authorities are required (according to Local Authority Circular (2000:13) to provide a **Personal Education Plan** (PEP) that '... ensures access to services and support; contributes to stability, minimises disruption and broken schooling; signals particular and special needs; establishes clear goals and acts as a record of progress and achievement.' The plan should:

- provide an achievement record (academic and otherwise);

- identify short-term targets; and

- establish long-term plans and aspirations.

Information about the child's education, including any special needs or statementing, should be given to you in the Child's Permanence Report (CPR).

Government guidance also requires that schools provide a "designated teacher" who oversees the education of looked after children. Statutory guidance, 'The role and responsibilities of the designated teacher for looked after children', makes clear that a child placed for adoption should be treated in the same way as any other looked after child for the purpose of school admission priority arrangements and in relation to the designated teacher's role, and since 2018 they have the same responsibilities to children who are adopted or previously looked after. Each local authority also has a Virtual Headteacher for looked after children, and they also have responsibilities for adopted children. They can help if there are difficulties, for example, with school admissions.

To help ensure continuity in meeting your child's educational needs after placement with you:

- check that information about their educational needs is contained in the Child's Permanence Report and adoption medical report;

- ask to review copies of your child's Care Plan and PEP and, where applicable, their EHC plan (see later in chapter);

- ask to speak to your child's teachers and/or designated teacher within his or her current nursery or school; and share the PEP and other relevant information with new staff or teachers, if your child is moving to a new school/nursery.

HELPFUL BOOKS

The Adopter's Handbook on Education, by Eileen Fursland, CoramBAAF, 2018
This handbook for adoptive parents provides information and advice to help adopters help their child to get the most out of school. It explores the education system, how parents can work with school staff to help them understand their child's needs and behaviours, and the kinds of innovative programmes that are helping schools to become more "attachment-aware".

Attachment in the Classroom: The links between children's early experience, emotional wellbeing and performance in school by Heather Geddes, Worth Publishing, 2006
Explores the significance of the relationship between the pupil, the teacher and the learning task, linking it to emotional development, behaviour and attachment experiences.

Nutmeg Gets into Trouble by Judith Foxon, BAAF, 2006
An illustrated story book which explores some of the problems adopted children may have at school.

Should I tell the school/teachers about my child's background?

Whether or not you choose to share details of your child's background with school staff is your own choice. Some parents may fear that their child will be treated "differently" if teachers know he or she is adopted, or that other children will ostracise the child if they discover anything about that child's background. However, in order to access the **Pupil Premium** grant, the school will need to be aware that your child is adopted.

You might find that sharing selected details with school staff will help them treat your child appropriately during certain portions of the school curriculum, such as studying family history or family trees.

If your child has significant academic or socialisation problems that affect his or her schooling, then you will most likely have to share some details of the adoption with school staff. Often, open communication with teachers will help them work with your child in an appropriate and helpful manner.

TERMS YOU MAY NEED TO KNOW

The local education authority or LEA is now sometimes referred to as the local authority. To avoid confusion, we have used the term education department or authority interchangeably, to distinguish it from the local authority as a whole, but where terms like named LEA officer are still current, we have retained them.

Academy school Academy schools are state-funded schools in England that are directly funded by the Department for Education and independent of local authority control. The terms of the arrangements are set out in individual Academy Funding Agreements. Most academies are secondary schools.

Education, Health and Care Plan (EHC) Assessment This is an assessment leading to an EHC plan for children from birth to 25 years old, for children who need more help than the usual provision of special educational needs support. It can be requested by parents or teachers of children with special educational needs.

Independent school A school neither maintained by a local education authority (LEA), nor a grant maintained school, but registered under the Education Act 1944. Section 189 of the Education Act 1993 gives the conditions under which an independent school may be approved by the Secretary of State as being suitable for the admission of children with statements of Special Educational Needs. Children attending these schools are not elibible to receive the Pupil Premium.

Individual Education Plan (IEP) A written document, prepared by school staff for children with special educational needs, which lists specific goals a child should aim to achieve during a named school term. The goals in an IEP can include educational achievements, as well as improvements in social skills. Parents and older children can participate in writing the IEP.

Learning Support Unit (LSU) A classroom provided to support disengaged pupils with difficult or challenging behaviour. The LSU may offer an alternative individual curriculum and behaviour packages, and may also offer individual counselling. The goal of the LSU is to enable students to return to mainstream school as quickly as possible.

Learning Support Assistant (LSA) A person who helps children who are in mainstream school, but who require extra learning support. LSAs are not specially trained, but are supported by the teacher and sometimes by visiting specialists.

Non-maintained special school Schools in England approved by the Secretary of State as special schools which are not maintained by the state, but charge fees on a non-profit-making basis. Most non-maintained special schools are run by major charities or charitable trusts.

Pupil Premium This is a grant paid to mainstream schools or academies to raise the attainment of disadvantaged pupils of all abilities to reach their potential. Looked after and adopted children are eligible for this grant, currently £1,900 per year. The school decides how to spend the grant, but this can be in consultation with the local authority and the child's parents.

Special Educational Needs Co-ordinator (SENCo) A teacher, appointed by the head teacher, who co-ordinates the services required for all children in the school who have special educational needs. This person can serve as a liaison between parents and the education department.

Special Education Needs and Disability Information Advice and Support Service (SENDIAS) These services replaced Parent Partnerships in response to the Children and Families Act 2014. They provide advice and information to children with SEN and their parents, including matters relating to health and social care.

Special school 'A school which is specially organised to make special educational provision for pupils with special educational needs and is, for the time being approved by the Secretary of State under section 188 of the Education Act 1993'.

Statements have been replaced with EHCs (see above) and from 1 September 2014, children with existing Statements were started to be transferred to EHC plans. All children have to undergo an EHC needs assessment before this transition can be completed, and all children should have been transitioned by 1 April 2018.

How do I choose a good school for my child?

Children adopted from care have priority access to schools, which means that your child should be able to attend whichever school you think best meets their needs (www.gov.uk/schools-admissions). They are also entitled to free early education from the age of two (tinyurl.com/first4early).

In addition to the usual considerations you have when choosing a school for your child, you may also have to think about the following questions if your child has learning and/or emotional behavioural difficulties.

- Does this school have experience of dealing with learning difficulties or emotional/behavioural difficulties?

- Does this school have the physical and/or financial resources needed to address learning or emotional/behavioural difficulties?

- Does the school specifically state it can handle emotional/behavioural difficulties?

- Can I communicate easily and comfortably with teachers and with the head teacher?

- How large is the school? Smaller class size and higher teacher to student ratios may make a smaller school easier for some adopted children. A small school, however, may not have the financial and/or physical resources that your child might require.

Independent schools are not subject to LEA regulations regarding special educational needs (see below) as are state-supported schools. You may find that some independent schools offer specific resources for children with "special needs". You should ask the school for its definition of "special needs" – sometimes these are defined only as learning difficulties and do not include emotional/behavioural difficulties.

What are "special educational needs and disabilities"?

"Special educational needs and disabilities" (SEND) include a broad range of problems that affect children at school – from specific learning difficulties to emotional/behavioural problems and developmental problems. The Department for Education (DfE) Code of Practice (2015) provides the following definition of special educational needs:

> *A child is defined as having special educational needs if he or she has a learning difficulty or disability which calls for special educational provision to be made for him or her. A learning difficulty means that the child has significantly greater difficulty in learning than the majority*

*of others of the same age. Or, it means a child has a disability which
prevents or hinders him or her from making use of facilities of a kind
generally provided for children of the same age in mainstream schools
or mainstream post-16 institutions.*

Identifying and addressing special educational needs should occur in three
distinct phases, according to the DfE Code of Practice:

1 Using existing school resources: if your child has difficulty at school, for
example, difficulty following instructions, paying attention, or writing
down information, the Code of Practice requires the school to address
the problem using its existing resources, such as a classroom assistant or
different teaching strategies.

2 If your child does not make progress, despite the support received from
school, the school can consult external services (within education or other
services) for specialist strategies or materials.

3 If progress is not made, then your child is entitled to a statutory
assessment of SEND by the local authority education department. This
usually involves your child completing a series of tests administered by an
educational psychologist. The education department must comply with a
request for an assessment unless it has already assessed the child within
the last six months or if it decides an assessment is not necessary. Parents
can appeal against this decision.

Education, Health and Care Plans

An Education, Health and Care Plan (EHCP) is for children and young
people aged up to 25 who need more support than the usual provision of
special educational needs support in school.

An EHCP identifies the child's educational, health and social needs and
sets out the additional support that should be provided to meet those
needs.

Requesting an EHC assessment

A request to the local authority for an assessment can be made by
teachers, parents and other people, including doctors. A young person is
entitled to request an assessment themselves if they are aged 16 to 25.

If the local authority decides to carry out an assessment, you may be
asked for:

• any reports from your child's school, nursery or childminder;

• medical assessments of your child;

- a letter from you about your child's needs.

The local authority will tell you within 16 weeks whether an EHCP is going to be made for your child.

Independent supporters can help you and your child through the SEN assessment process. Your SENCO can provide more information, or you can contact your local Special Educational Needs and Disability Information and Advice Service (SENDIAS).

Understanding your child's entitlements to special education provision

SEND Code of Practice (2015) – provides schools and local authorities (LAs) with a framework for making decisions about various aspects of special educational needs – it provides general guidance, but does not dictate what LAs must do in individual cases. The Code of Practice was revised based on the requirements of Part 3 of the Children and Families Act 2014, which came into force on 1 September 2014.

SEND tribunal – a judicial body to which parents can appeal for any of the following reasons:

- if the LA decides not to assess their child for SEND;

- if the LA assesses the child, but decides not to issue an EHC Plan;

- if parents disagree with the LA's decision about what SEND help the child needs;

- or if the LA tries to withdraw the child's Plan, but the parents think the child still needs it.

The tribunal's decision is binding on the LA, regardless of the cost or resources required to meet the child's needs. The SEND tribunal is required to follow the SEND Code of Practice when making its decisions.

Government Guidance

- *Mental Health and Behaviour in Schools* (DfE, March 2016) provides advice for schools on managing behaviour and their responsibilities.

- *Special Educational Needs and Disability: A guide for parents and carers* (DfE, August 2014) sets out information for parents about the system for children and young people paged 0–25 with SEN or a disability.

HELPFUL ORGANISATIONS

Contact your local authority to find out if it produces a Parents' Information Guide about schools in your area and their services, including special educational needs. Some LAs or councils also have a website that provides such information.

Information on special educational needs

ACE Education Advice & ACE Education Training

Provides information about all aspects of state education, and helps parents who are dealing with schools or education authorities. Has a number of booklets and briefings available as free downloads.

72 Durnsford Road
London N11 2EJ
Advice line: 0300 0115142
www.ace-ed.org.uk

Caspari Foundation

Established in 2000, this organisation promotes educational therapy and therapeutic learning to help children who have emotional barriers that can impair learning. Provides courses for teachers, as well as consultations for children and their parents.

Finspace
225–229 Seven Sisters Road
London N4 2DA
Tel: 020 7527 5161
www.caspari.org.uk

Children in Scotland

Provides a national information and advice service for parents, professionals, children and young people living in Scotland who have questions about special educational needs.

Level 1 Rosebery House
7 Haymarket Terrace
Edinburgh EH12 5EZ
Tel: 0131 313 2322

Email: info@childreninscotland.org.uk
www.childreninscotland.org.uk

Enquire

Scottish advice service for additional support for learning.

Helpline: 0345 123 2303
www.enquire.org.uk

Coram Children's Legal Centre, Education and Advocacy Unit

Provides advice and representation to children and/or parents involved in education disputes with a school or a local education authority. The Unit operates within the south-east of England. For education disputes outside this area, the Centre can provide advice, as well as negotiation and mediation.

Head office
Riverside Office Centre
Century House North
North Station Road
Colchester CO1 1RE
Tel: 01206 714650
www.childrenslegalcentre.com

Department for Education (DfE)

Provides information for parents about all aspects of education and schools. The DfE website offers a Parents' Centre that provides specific and comprehensive information about SEN. Contact the DfE publications department to find out about specific information for parents, such as the SEN Guide for Parents, and for a copy of the Code of Practice.

DfE Publications
Tel: 0845 602 2260
www.education.gov.uk

Independent Panel for Special Education Advice (IPSEA)

A charity that aims to ensure that children with special educational needs receive the special education provision to which they are legally entitled. Provides free, independent advice; free advice on appealing to the SEND Tribunal (including representation, if needed) and second opinions from professionals.

24–26 Gold Street
Saffron Walden CB10 1SJ
www.ipsea.org.uk

The Institute for Arts in Therapy and Education

A college of higher education dedicated to in-depth theoretical and practical study of artistic, imaginative and emotional expression, and the understanding and enhancement of emotional well-being.

2–18 Britannia Row
London N1 8PA
Tel: 020 7704 2534
www.artspsychotherapy.org

National Association for Special Educational Needs (NASEN)

Promotes the education, training, advancement and development of people with special educational needs. Services to members include several regular publications and regional courses and conferences.

4–5 Amber Business Village
Amber Close, Amington
Tamworth
B77 4RP
Tel: 01827 311 500
Email: welcome@nasen.org.uk
www.nasen.org.uk

PAC UK Education Service

Provides training and resources for schools, social workers and parents and guardians of adopted children.

www.pac-uk.org/education

School Health Service

Identifies and assesses children who have physical, emotional or behavioural problems. It includes a named school nurse and paediatric doctors who have additional training to help with school services. The Health Service provides advice to LAs and offers specialist services, such as for enuresis (bedwetting) clinics, audiology services and for emotional difficulties. Contact your local authority to find phone numbers for your local School Health Teams.

SENAC – Special Educational Needs Advice Centre

Provides an independent advice, information and advocacy service for parents of children and young people with special educational needs.
Advice line: 028 9079 5779
www.senac.co.uk

Special Educational Consortium

Convened under the auspices of the Council for Disabled Children to protect and promote the interest of disabled children and children with special educational needs.

c/o National Children's Bureau
8 Wakley Street
London EC1V 7QE
Tel: 020 7843 6049
Email: jritson@ncb.org.uk
www.councilfordisabledchildren.org.uk/special-educational-consortium

Information about learning difficulties

British Institute for Learning Disabilities (BILD)

Works to improve the quality of life for all people with a learning disability. It conducts research into various aspects of learning disabilities, and provides information and services for people with learning disabilities, their families and professionals.

Birmingham Research Park
97 Vincent Drive

Edgbaston
Birmingham B15 2SQ
Tel: 0121 415 6960
Email: enquiries@bild.org.uk
www.bild.org.uk

The Institute for Neuro-phsyiological Psychology (INPP)
Established in 1975 to research the effects of central nervous system dysfunction on learning difficulties in children and on adults suffering from neuroses. Contact the institute for further information about its services and its fees.

1 Stanley Street, Chester CH1 2LR
Tel: 01244 311 414
www.inpp.org.uk

The Mental Health Foundation
Provides information and support for people and families who have any type of mental health problem and/or learning disability. Included within the MHF is The Foundation for People with Learning Disabilities.

London office
Colechurch House
1 London Bridge Walk
London SE1 2SX
Tel: 020 7803 1100
www.mentalhealth.org.uk
www.learningdisabilities.org.uk

Scotland office
5th Floor, Merchants House
30 George Square
Glasgow G2 1EG
Tel: 0141 572 0125

Wales office
Castle Court
6 Cathedral Road
Cardiff CF11 9LJ
Tel: 02921 679400

Center for Positive Behavioural Intervention and Support
www.pbis.org
Created by the US Department for Education to help schools implement and sustain positive behaviour-intervention programmes.

Information about home schooling

Home Education Advisory Service (HEAS)
A UK-based national charity providing information and support for home education. Produces information, provides support for parents, and works with local authorities to monitor and inspect home education programmes.

PO Box 98
Welwyn Garden City
Hertfordshire AL8 6AN
Tel: 01707 371 854
Email: enquiries@heas.org.uk
www.heas.org.uk

Publications

The Adopter's Handbook on Education by Eileen Fursland, CoramBAAF, 2018
This handbook for adoptive parents provides information and advice to help adopters help their child to get the most out of school. It explores the education system and how parents can work with school staff to help them understand their child's needs and behaviours.

Learn the Child: Helping looked after children to learn (second edition) by Kate Cairns and Chris Stanway, BAAF, 2013
A training resource for social workers, carers and teachers on helping looked after children to learn. It could also be helpful to adoptive parents.

Learning Disabilities in Children by Peter Burke and Katy Cigno, Blackwell Science, 2000.
Explains how learning difficulties are defined and examines their impact on family life. The book is aimed at those working in child welfare, social work and community care.

The Mental Health of Looked After and Adopted Children by Karen Aldred and Helen Rodwell, CoramBAAF, 2018
This comprehensive and holistic practice guide, aimed at social workers, explores children's mental health, focusing in particular on conditions common to looked after children.

Mental Health and Behaviour in Schools
A booklet produced by the Department for Education (DfE) to provide advice for teachers and other school staff. It explores how to support children with emotional and behavioural difficulties, strengthening pupil resilience, how to identify pupils likely to need extra support, and how to access community and CAMHS support. Available at: www.gov.uk/government/publications/mental-health-and-behaviour-in-schools--2

Education Health and Care Needs Assessment
Explains the assessment process for an EHC Plan, and gives advice for parents on making a request for an assessment and preparing a report about their child for the local authority. Available from ACE Education Advice at: www.ace-ed.org.uk/.

SEND: A guide for parents and carers
Available free from the Department for Education at: www.gov.uk/government/publications/send-guide-for-parents-and-carers.

Special Educational Needs and Disability (SEND)
Provides a range of updates and Government documents about SEND, aimed at schools, social care professionals and health professionals. Available at: www.gov.uk/topic/schools-colleges-childrens-services/special-educational-needs-disabilities.

Your child: physical and emotional needs

In this section

→ learn about the general effects of trauma and neglect on children

→ examine the emotional and physical difficulties adopted children may experience

→ find out how to access the services your child may need and how to ensure your child receives the help to which he or she is entitled

→ gather information about the organisations and resources which can help you and your child with particular difficulties

Introduction

Children in need of adoption and fostering will have experienced separation from their birth families. These children, *regardless of their age*, will be affected (to varying degrees) by that separation. In addition to the effects of separation and loss, many of these children may also have experienced varying degrees of trauma as a result of neglect and/or abuse.

Many of us are generally familiar with the *physical* impact of neglect and abuse on children. However, it is important to be aware that the *emotional* effects of early trauma may be less obvious, but equally profound. The repercussions of this trauma can deeply affect your child, no matter at what age you adopted him or her.

Today there are many resources and services to help children who have physical, emotional and developmental difficulties as a result of early trauma. The purpose of this section, therefore, is to give you a basic understanding of the possible needs your adopted child may have, so that you can find the services and information to meet your child's needs.

Varying degrees...what does it mean?

The phrase "varying degrees" applies to all of the problems discussed in this section. Every child is an individual and your adopted child may – or may not – experience the difficulties presented here. There are many factors that determine how extensively a child is affected by emotional or physical trauma. These include the age of the child when he or she experienced the trauma and the length of time the child experienced the trauma. Younger children are less likely to be affected as deeply as older children – but even children adopted as infants can show the effects of early trauma later in life.

It may be difficult for you – or for the professionals involved with your adoption – to determine exactly how much your child may be affected by past experiences and what needs your child may have now or in the future. But you will be able to help yourself and your child if you are aware of potential difficulties that may arise, and know where to seek appropriate help if you need it.

Possible effects of neglect and/or abuse on children

Abuse and neglect of children can take several forms. The word "abuse" commonly refers to a clearly identifiable event or series of events in a child's life, whereas "neglect" refers to an ongoing experience of deprivation. "Abuse", however, can sometimes be used to cover both situations, so it is important to be clear about what has actually happened to a child. A common image of children in the care system is of children who have been sexually or physically abused. Yet many of them are being looked after solely as a result of neglect of their basic needs and such neglect can sometimes damage a child more than individual episodes of abuse.

Regardless of how it occurs, neglect and abuse are **traumatic events** for a child. You may often hear health professionals refer to children experiencing trauma or being traumatised – a word defined in medical circles as meaning 'an emotionally painful and harmful event that sometimes leads to long-term mental health difficulties'. It is this trauma that creates the emotional wounds that may take many years (or even a lifetime) to resolve.

What information can I find from the child's health records?

Your child's social worker is required by law to give you full information in writing about your child when the agency first approaches you about a child (the Child's Permanence Report). This will include a summary of the child's health information by the medical adviser. The initial health assessment of your child will record physical and emotional development and needs, and will also indicate any issues that should be followed up. A copy of the health assessment report will be sent to your child's GP as well as to you. It is sensible to discuss this either with your GP or with the agency's medical adviser who may have carried out the assessment and who will in any case submit comments on it to the adoption court. The making of an adoption order does not prevent you from consulting your adoption agency and its medical adviser if you have any concerns about your child's health. You may also ask your GP to consult the agency on your behalf.

Your child's health assessment may include information about his or her birth parents. It is important to remember that this information, whether given or implied, must be treated as strictly confidential, privy only to yourselves as parents, to your child's GP, to the adoption court and, when he or she is older, to your child.

It is good practice for the medical adviser to meet with the prospective adopter to share all appropriate health information, to discuss the needs of the child with whom they are matched, and to provide a written report of this meeting.

What physical and/or developmental issues might we have to deal with?

Symptoms of neglect or abuse can include, for example, severe nappy rash, inadequate and unexplained weight gain or loss, withdrawn behaviour (or its opposite, indiscriminate displays of affection), unexplained bruises and a history of frequent visits to hospital accident and emergency departments. Health visitors, doctors, social workers, teachers and others involved with the child can initiate action on the child's behalf to deal with the situation, which for some children may include being looked after by the local authority. A child's physical and emotional development will often improve with placement in a secure and loving environment, although in many cases this will take months, or even longer.

There may be some physical and developmental problems that do *not* go away after the child is placed with you or which may take many years to overcome. Some of these difficulties, such as small size, can result from poor antenatal care, as well as neglect after the child is born. These are difficulties, therefore, that you may have to deal with as adoptive parents.

Physical issues

In addition to any diagnosed conditions the child might have been born with (e.g. Down's syndrome, asthma, other physical disabilities), the child may have general difficulties, such as small size (height and weight) for his or her age. Some children may have problems with wetting and soiling (day and/or night), due to their early experiences. It will be important for you to work closely with your health visitor and/or GP to help your child with these issues. Although these issues will improve over time, your child may never completely overcome some of them.

Developmental issues

Children who have been neglected do not always develop the same "skills" as other children of their age. Neglected children, for example, may not learn how to understand language; they may be slow in learning how to walk or run, how to throw a ball, how to use the toilet, or how to eat as expected for their age. These are only a few of the skills a neglected child may not learn. The extent to which a child develops skills will differ with each individual and will also depend on the extent and timescale of the neglect.

What does "delayed" mean?

Your child's development may well be described as "delayed". It is often unclear whether this is due to the abuse and neglect they have suffered or whether their development is affected due to other reasons. The term "delay" may indicate that eventually the child will catch up in their development. This may happen with all the good care which you are able to give. However, it may not – and you must be prepared for the fact that your child's development may always be affected to some extent and in some aspects.

Possible developmental delays due to neglect can include:

- delayed language skills

- limited attention span

- delayed motor skills

- learning difficulties

- immature behaviour for his or her age

- immature behaviour when interacting with other children

- lack of self-esteem

- inability to control emotions (anger and joy)

Most children learn many of these skills and, with time, catch up to their age level when they are placed in a nurturing environment. If you are unsure of your child's physical and/or developmental status when he or she is placed with you, it may be helpful to arrange a visit to your health visitor or child development clinic for assistance. Some children may have learning difficulties resulting from developmental delay. Some of these may not be noticed until the child reaches school age.

Developmental delay: chicken or egg?

It may be difficult to determine whether or not a child's difficulties are caused by physical, developmental or emotional problems. If your eight-year-old son wets himself at school, for example, is this problem due to a delay in his bladder development, previous experiences, distraction by other children at school, or the distance he has to travel to use the school toilets? Sometimes, all of these factors contribute to a child's problems. Thus, many parents don't know where to look for help.

A good place to begin is with your GP and/or health visitor. If required, they may refer you to the local child development or paediatric service.

What physical, emotional and/or mental health issues might you have to deal with?

Issues the child may be born with

Neglected or abused children may have different types of health difficulties that are not a direct result of neglect or abuse; for example, congenital conditions such as heart disease. If such conditions are already diagnosed in the child (or if there is an inherited problem that exists in members of the birth family but currently not in the child), you should be fully informed by social workers and medical advisers. In rare cases, a congenital condition becomes apparent some time after a child's adoption. In such situations adoptive parents are advised to contact their adoption agency in the interests of members of their child's birth family.

The developing foetus can also be damaged if the mother was a heavy smoker or drinker, took harmful drugs or neglected herself and her diet.

Foetal alcohol spectrum disorder (FASD)

This term describes a wide range of disorders affecting children whose birth mother misused alcohol during pregnancy. This is an umbrella term that also includes foetal alcohol syndrome (FAS) or foetal alcohol effects (FAE). It is not clear what level of alcohol use – including timing in the pregnancy, volume, frequency and duration – can trigger structural damage to the brain in unborn babies. Characteristics of foetal alcohol syndrome often include abnormalities of growth, a weakened immune system, and certain facial features. Children with some, but not all, of these characteristics are said to have foetal alcohol effects. Most babies with FASD will seem irritable, have trouble eating and sleeping, and may be sensitive to sensory stimulation. They may also have some level of developmental delay and learning difficulties at a later stage. FASD cannot be "cured", but with consistency, support and loving care, children can be helped to understand and live with their condition.

HELPFUL BOOKS

Parenting a Child Affected by Parental Substance Misuse by Donald Forrester, BAAF, 2012
Part of CoramBAAF's Parenting Matters series of short guides for parents and carers, this book includes accessible information about the effects on children of parental substance misuse, along with accounts from parents describing what it is like to parent an affected child.

Children Exposed to Parental Substance Misuse: Implications for family placement edited by Rena Phillips, BAAF, 2004
An informative anthology which looks at the effects of tobacco, drugs and alcohol on the foetus, the newborn and the infant.

Holding on and Hanging in by Lorna Miles, BAAF, 2010
Tracks Wayne's journey from first being fostered by Lorna when he was nine years old, having been neglected and affected by domestic abuse and parental alcohol and substance misuse, through nearly four years of family life in a therapeutic placement.

Problems resulting from abuse or neglect

Children needing adoption may experience a range of mental health problems that are a direct result of abuse and/or neglect. These difficulties can be emotional and/or behavioural, and may include poor self-image and self-esteem; overly aggressive and/or attention-seeking behaviour; inability to form genuine attachment relationships with other adults and/or children; anxious or "vigilant" behaviour; indiscriminate physical contact with strangers; inability to concentrate; lack of sense of "personal space"; and self-injuring or self-stimulating behaviours (e.g. masturbation).

HELPFUL ORGANISATIONS

NOFAS UK (National Organisation on Foetal Alcohol Syndrome UK)
Committed to helping individuals affected by FASD and providing specialist services.

022 Southbank House
Black Prince Road
London SE1 7SJ

Tel: 020 8458 5951
Helpline: 08700 333 700
Email: info@nofas-uk.org
www.nofas-uk.org

DrugWise
The UK's leading independent centre of expertise on drugs and drug use.

www.drugwise.org.uk

Attachment difficulties

This is one of the main problems for children who have experienced abuse, neglect and the trauma of separation. Attachment, briefly described, is the process of emotional bonding that occurs between infants and their main caregiver (usually mothers) during the first months and several years of life. During this period the infant learns many aspects of emotions and socialisation from his or her caregiver and forms a secure, loving relationship with that person.

So what happens in infants and children who do not have this connection with a main caregiver? Research now indicates that lack of physical contact, stimulation and communication with a main caregiver can inhibit the child from developing social behaviours (such as sharing, learning right and wrong, etc) that he or she would have learned from the caregiver. It is now known that this lack of contact also affects the growth and development of certain areas of the brain. This then leads to a lack of emotional development (such as knowing how to express emotions verbally, e.g. 'I feel sad'). Children who have not formed an attachment to a main caregiver(s) are described by health professionals as suffering from "attachment difficulties".

This guide provides only a brief description of attachment difficulties in children. The good news is that there is a growing body of literature and support to help parents and children. Current research shows, for example, that the physical development of the brain can occur throughout life, once the child receives the appropriate stimulation and attachment to a main caregiver.

The difficult news is that children don't overcome attachment difficulties overnight. It takes a lot of perseverance, patience and determination from parents to help children overcome such problems.

HELPFUL BOOKS

Attachment, Trauma and Resilience by Kate and Brian Cairns, CoramBAAF, 2016
Kate, Brian and three birth children have fostered 12 children who remain part of their family. They draw on the wealth of their personal and professional experience to offer a vivid glimpse into life with children who have experienced attachment difficulties, abuse and trauma, and shows in a range of everyday situations how the family responded.

Together in Time by Ruth and Ed Royce, BAAF, 2008
Ruth and Ed look back on their decision to adopt a boy with attachment difficulties, the fear that their family was falling apart, and their experience of music and art therapy.

Promoting Attachment and Resilience: A guide for foster carers and adopters on using the Secure Base Model by Gillian Schofield and Mary Beek, BAAF, 2014
Secure Base is a widely respected model of caregiving based on theories of attachment and resilience while also drawing on child placement research. This practical guide is designed to support parents and carers in providing a secure base for children who have experienced trauma and loss. An accompanying DVD provides further information.

Post-Traumatic Stress Disorder (PTSD) is a condition that may affect children and adults who have experienced extreme physical or psychological trauma. Thus, children who have suffered intense abuse or neglect or witnessed severe violence or, in some cases, experienced a sudden removal from a loved carer or familiar environment, may have difficulties with PTSD.

People who have PTSD suffer recurrent memories of the traumatic stress, rather than being able to "integrate" the traumatic experience into the normal cycle of emotional recovery. When the flashes of traumatic memory occur, the body experiences the same physical and psychological stress as if the event were actually occurring. This leads to physical and behavioural reactions, such as increased heart rate and breathing, sweating, panic, nightmares, eating disorders, aggression and hyperactivity. When a child's body and mind are continually bombarded by such stress, it affects the child's ability to recover a healthy emotional state. The child's behavioural responses to the stress affect his or her ability to socialise, to learn (thus to attend school) and to participate in family life and other "normal" childhood activities. Children who suffer from PTSD should receive professional medical and psychological help.

Attention Deficit Hyperactivity Disorder (ADHD) is an impairment of activity and attention control. The diagnostic features are inattention, over-activity (especially in situations requiring calm) and impulsiveness.

Children who have been neglected or abused often display anxious and hyperactive behaviour as a result of insecure emotional attachment. This behaviour may sometimes be interpreted as ADHD or ADD (Attention Deficit Disorder). There is a great deal of controversy about these conditions and whether children diagnosed with ADHD or ADD actually have attachment difficulties rather than ADHD/ADD, or vice versa. It is important to be aware of these issues if you need to consult health professionals about your child's behaviour (see Appendix 2 for ADD organisations).

HELPFUL BOOKS

Parenting a Child with Attention Deficit Hyperactivity Disorder by Brian Jacobs and Lorna Miles, BAAF, 2012
Part of BAAF's Parenting Matters series of short guides for parents and carers, this book includes accessible information about the effects on children of Attention Deficit Hyperactivity Disorder, along with accounts from parents describing what it is like to care for an affected child.

CoramBAAF's Parenting Matters series also includes titles on emotional and behavioural difficulties, autism spectrum disorder, developmental delay, mental health issues, dyslexia, genetic disorders, emotional and behavioural difficulties, trauma, domestic violence and sexual abuse.

Obtaining health services for your child

Health services for babies, children and adolescents are provided by a range of professionals in both hospital and the community. The health visitor has a helpful role in health promotion and in identifying the health care needs of under-fives and in helping to ensure access to the services necessary to meet those needs. Health organisations are obliged, under section 10 of the Education Act 1981, to inform parents of children under five of any relevant voluntary organisation which could help with a childhood disability or learning difficulty. This means that health organisations should keep information about local self-help groups, etc, in order to provide effective information services.

Every child born since 1992 has a **Personal Child Health Record** – make sure you obtain this from your social worker or voluntary agency. If this record cannot be located, ask your local health visitor or GP to arrange for a new one to be made for your child. There are often delays in securing health records of children who have had several moves from area to area

HELPFUL BOOKS

The Adopter's Handbook on Therapy by Eileen Fursland, CoramBAAF, 2016
This practical handbook provides clear and factual information on what therapy is, what the different therapies and therapeutic parenting support programmes entail, and what behaviours and issues each can help with, along with personal accounts from adopters who have benefited from some of these approaches.

Promoting the Health of Children in Public Care edited by Florence Merredew and Carolyn Sampeys, BAAF, 2015
This anthology is a guide to good practice in promoting the health of looked after and adopted children, and provides expert advice on many aspects of physical and mental health. Although aimed at health and social work professionals, it contains much information that could be of use to adopters and carers.

or who have a complicated medical history including hospital treatment. You may need to encourage your GP or hospital to persist in chasing these records. Sometimes the child's change of name presents a barrier to be negotiated, and your adoption agency's medical adviser should be able to help you with this.

The Carer Held Health Record produced by CoramBAAF is specifically designed for carers of looked after children who may have frequent moves, to supplement the Personal Child Health Record. It should be kept confidentially by adults caring for the child and should accompany the child when s/he moves.

Community health services for children – these services can include: audiology, child development assistance, occupational therapy, physiotherapy, school health services, services for children with a learning disability, and speech and language therapy, in addition to other services. Services may include a **Learning Disability Nursing Team** whose nurses have specialist training to work with children who have a learning disability. They can provide help, support and advice, such as developing relationship and life skills, and with continence and physical or sensory disabilities. Contact your GP or your local health organisations for details of this service in your area.

Health Link Worker (usually a named health visitor or named school health adviser) can co-ordinate services needed by pre-school and school-aged children who require extra health care.

HELPFUL TRAINING COURSES AND BOOKS

Training Courses

Parenting our Children

This course devised by Adoption UK is available to parents through local authorities and can be funded by the Adoption Support Fund (ASF). The programme is designed to help parents develop understanding and expertise in dealing with attachment issues and the effects of early trauma in children. Parents explore their own expectations and share new and creative parenting strategies.

Enhancing Adoptive Parenting: A parenting manual for use with new adopters of challenging children

by Alan Rushton and Helen Upright, BAAF, 2012

This parenting manual is written for adoption support workers and intended to make practical and relevant advice available to the many struggling adopters. The programme aims to support the stability of the adoptive placement, to reduce the level of child problems, and enhance parenting skills and understanding, and improve relationships.

Leaflets, booklets, guides

Attachment Handbook for Foster Care and Adoption by Gillian Schofield and Mary Beek, 2nd edition, CoramBAAF, 2018

A comprehensive book that describes different types of attachment, attachment formation and development, and how children can be helped to form new attachments in foster and adoptive families.

Attachment, Trauma and Resilience: Therapeutic caring for children

by Kate and Brian Cairns, CoramBAAF, 2016

Offers a vivid picture of family life with children who have experienced attachment difficulties, loss, abuse and trauma and how the family responded.

Building the Bonds of Attachment by Daniel Hughes, Jason Aronson, 2006

Critically acclaimed book for those who strive to assist poorly attached children, which blends attachment theory, research, and trauma theory with general principles of parenting and family therapy to develop a model for intervention.

Connecting with Kids through Stories: Using narratives to facilitate attachment in adopted children by Denise Lacher, Todd Nichols and Joanne May, Jessica Kingsley Publishers, 2012

An accessible guide to family attachment narrative therapy for the parents of adopted or fostered children.

Trauma, Attachment and Family Permanence: Fear can stop you loving

edited by Caroline Archer and Alan Burnell, Jessica Kingsley Publishers, 2003

Draws on the programmes offered by Family Futures to explore the challenges faced by the professional or parent who seeks to promote family permanence. Brings together a rich selection of ideas.

Looking after the emotional health of children in foster care and in residential care

In 1996, the National Children's Bureau undertook a three-year project to identify the mental health needs of children in foster or residential care. The study found that carers are concerned about the mental health of the children in their care and that there is a lack of mental health support for carers from local health authorities. As a result of studies in Glasgow, researchers have concluded that, 'A better understanding of the emotional and behavioural difficulties experienced by many looked after children is crucial if appropriate interventions are to be provided. The first step towards this is for every child entering care to have a comprehensive psychological assessment so their individual needs can be identified and met.'*

The House of Commons Education Committee produced a report in 2016 on the mental health and wellbeing of looked after children. They raised concerns about the assessment of children's mental health and services being provided, and they also recommended that all looked after children should have a full mental health assessment by a qualified mental health professional.

Won't there be extra "emotional hurdles" for my adopted child as he or she grows up?

Yes. In addition to the possible problems with self-esteem and attachment mentioned earlier, children may have questions about their life history and about their birth family, to varying degrees. The way in which these issues affect your child may be influenced by the child's age at adoption and by the amount of contact he or she has with the birth family. Very young children usually happily accept the story of their adoption, but as they grow old enough to understand the concept of rejection, some children become anxious or withdrawn when adoption is mentioned. Extra sensitivity is required if this seems to be happening. Help is available with this kind of difficulty, so do not hesitate to seek it if you feel uncertain about how to handle it. These issues can affect a child's behaviour without you – or your child – realising it.

It is important to talk openly with your child about his or her life history, and to provide the facts, little by little, as your child becomes old enough to understand them. Many adoptive parents help their children talk about their life history using the life story book provided by their social worker (see Section 1). Talking about these events openly and in a positive manner will help your child understand his or her life history and come to terms with any difficult issues. There are many resources and organisations that can help both you and your child along the way.

---

* H. Minnis and C. Del Priori, 'Mental health services for looked after children: implications from two studies', *Adoption & Fostering*, 25: 4, pp 27–38.

HELPFUL ORGANISATIONS

Meeting your child's physical, developmental, emotional and/or behavioural needs

In addition to the post-adoption support services described in Section 5, the following organisations may provide information and assistance.

The Anna Freud Centre

A registered charity that provides services to families and children with emotional, behavioural, and developmental difficulties. The Centre also conducts research into the effectiveness of psychotherapy techniques and children's emotional development, including attachment. Treatment is provided to families based on need, not on ability to pay.

12 Maresfield Gardens
London NW3 5SU
Tel: 020 7794 2313
www.annafreud.org

Association for Child and Adolescent Mental Health

An association for professionals of various disciplines who are involved with children. It arranges seminars and publishes professional journals. It does not provide an advice service.

St Saviour's House
39–41 Union Street
London SE1 1SD
Tel: 020 7403 7458
www.acamh.org.uk

Association of Child Psychotherapists (ACP)

A professional organisation for child psychotherapists in the UK. Recognised by the Department of Health as the body which accredits UK training in child and adolescent psychotherapy.

CAN Mezzanine
32-36 Loman Street
London SE1 0EH
Tel: 020 7922 7751
www.childpsychotherapy.org.uk

British Association for Counselling and Psychotherapy (BACP)

Provides details of local counsellors and psychotherapists online.

BACP House, 15 St John's Business Park
Lutterworth
Leicestershire LE17 4HB
Tel: 01455 883300 (information)
Email: bacp@bacp.co.uk
www.bacp.co.uk

British Psychotherapy Foundation

Provides training in psychotherapy and help with finding a psychotherapist.

37 Mapesbury Road
London NW2 4HJ
Tel: 020 8452 9823
www.britishpsychotherapyfoundation.org.uk

Caspari Foundation

Promotes educational therapy and therapeutic learning to help children who have emotional barriers that can impair learning. Provides courses for teachers, as well as consultations for children and their parents.

Finspace
225-229 Seven Sisters Road
London N4 2DA
Tel: 020 7527 5161
www.caspari.org.uk

The Centre for Child Mental Health
The aim of the centre is to expand awareness of emotional well-being and mental health of children. It conducts research in child mental health, provides information for parents, teachers, professionals and the public, and provides seminars by mental health professionals, covering a range of child mental health topics, including issues that affect adopted children.

2–18 Britannia Row
London N1 8PA
Tel: 020 7354 2913
www.childmentalhealthcentre.org

UCL Great Ormond Street Institute of Child Health
The largest paediatric training and research centre in the UK. The hospital offers the widest range of paediatric specialists in the country.

30 Guildford Street
London WC1N 1EH
Tel: 020 7242 9789
www.ucl.ac.uk/ich

YoungMinds
A children's mental health charity committed to improving the mental health of all children and young people. Provides information and services, as well as advocacy work within government and professional organisations; conducts training and seminars for professionals; and conducts consultancy work to develop services for children. Also provides information for young people, parents and professionals.

Suite 11 Baden Place
Crosby Row
London SE1 1YW
Tel: 020 7089 5050
Parents Helpline: 0808 802 5544
www.youngminds.org.uk

Can I ask the local authority for help after I have adopted my child?

Yes. Many local authorities are trying to keep in touch with adopters, as all voluntary adoption agencies do, by offering a regular newsletter, workshops, social events, etc. However, even if you are not in contact with a local authority, you can ask for help. If it is more than three years since your child was adopted, you should approach the local authority where you live. Otherwise, you should contact the local authority which placed your child with you. The Adoption Support Services Regulations 2005 impose a duty on local authorities to assess your needs and that of your child for adoption support at any time during his/her childhood.

All local authorities in England are required to have a range of adoption support services in their area. These are:

- financial support;
- support groups for adoptive parents and adopted children;

- support for contact arrangements between adopted children and their birth relatives or other important people;

- therapeutic services for children;

- training, respite care and other services to help support the placement;

- counselling, advice and information.

You and your child have a right to have an assessment of your needs for adoption support by the local authority, either those listed above or any others, e.g. help in liaising with schools, help in talking with the child about adoption, etc. The local authority must prepare a written adoption support plan which sets out what it has assessed your support needs are and how it proposes to meet these. Guidance to the regulations states that local authorities must act reasonably in deciding whether to provide adoption support services following an assessment. However, it may not be possible to provide a service to meet every need. You may be able to complain about or challenge "unreasonable" decisions.

Local authorities can now apply to the Adoption Support Fund (ASF) to provide funding for therapeutic support identified by their assessment.

Promoting the health and wellbeing of looked after children – revised statutory guidance

This was issued in March 2015. It is statutory on local authorities, Clinical Commissioning Groups (CCG) and NHS England. It applies in England only. It sets out a framework for effective joint working between these agencies and gives guidance on providing an effective service for looked after children and their carers, and the requirement for a Health Plan for all looked after children.

Is it more difficult to adopt a child who has a physical, mental or learning disability?

No. The process for adopting a child with a disability is the same as for any other child. Again, the main concern of the adoption agency will be that you are able to meet the specific needs of that child. Because a disabled child may place different and/or additional pressures on adoptive parents, there are many disabled children waiting for adoption. Many local authorities are proactive in trying to recruit adoptive parents for these children.

Under the NHS and Community Care Act 1990 and the Children Act 1989, children's services have a duty to assess the needs of a child with a disability. If you adopt a disabled child, you have the right to ask for your child's needs to be assessed by the children's services department and you also have the right to ask for an assessment for yourself – this will be under the Children and Families Act 2014. Once your child's needs have

HELPFUL GUIDES

What is a Disability?, by Hedi Argent, 2004. A guide for children that describes different disabilities and explains what they mean. Available from CoramBAAF (Appendix 1).

been assessed, the social worker will agree with you what services are to be provided.

These services could include practical assistance in the home; provision of recreational or educational facilities; home adaptations; travel, meals, and other assistance; a telephone and ancillary equipment. The provision of short breaks for parents of disabled children is governed by the Breaks for Carers of Disabled Children Regulations 2011. The Care Act 2014 sets out rights for families to be supported with their children's transition to adult services. Other services may be provided under the Children Act but these may be discretionary. You will need to find out what is available from your local authority. You can call the Contact helpline for more information or download their guide at https://contact.org.uk/media/1160983/introduction_to_the_care_act_2014_-_england.pdf.

Will we be more likely to receive financial support if we adopt a disabled child?

According to the Adoption Support Services Regulations 2005, financial support may be paid if the child 'needs special care which requires a greater expenditure of resources by reason of illness, disability, emotional or behavioural difficulties or the continuing consequences of past abuse or neglect'. You will be "assessed" for any financial support for which you may be eligible. For more information about financial support, see Section 2 of this handbook.

Families of disabled children may also be entitled to additional support, such as the disability living allowance. For more information about these allowances, contact your local benefits provider.

HELPFUL ORGANISATIONS

If your child has a physical or mental difficulty

There are many organisations which support children with specific difficulties. Those listed here are "umbrella" organisations that provide general support regarding adoption and/or physical or mental difficulties.

Contact

Provides guidance and information for parents on over 2,000 rare medical conditions, including information about support groups. There is also a freephone helpline for parents seeking information regarding help for disabled children.

209-211 City Road
London EC1V 1JN
Helpline: 0808 808 3555
Tel: 020 7608 8700
Textphone: 0808 808 3556
Email: info@contact.org.uk
www.contact.org.uk

Council for Disabled Children

Promotes collaborative work between different organisations providing services and support for children and young people with disabilities and special educational needs. Offers a range of services, including consultancy, training, information, publications and conferences.

8 Wakley Street
London EC1V 7QE
Tel: 020 7843 1900
email: cdc@ncb.org.uk
www.councilfordisabledchildren.org.uk

PUBLICATIONS

Supporting the Mental Health of Looked After and Adopted Children by Helen Rodwell and Karen Aldred, CoramBAAF, 2018

This Good Practice Guide explores children's mental health from a holistic perspective, considering how to take into account the effect of children's life history and circumstances. The second half of the book looks at different mental health problems and the ways in which they may affect children.

Every Child is Special: Placing disabled children for permanence by Jennifer Cousins, BAAF, 2006

This Good Practice Guide considers permanence planning for disabled children and recruitment and assessment of families. It highlights the changes that are necessary if more disabled children are to have the security of a permanent family.

The Family Business by Robert Marsden, BAAF, 2008

A story of the adoption of William, a little boy with cerebral palsy, by a middle-aged couple with three birth children.

When your Child has Additional Needs: A guide to help and support for parents of a disabled child Contact, 2013

An extremely useful online guide that gives pointers to the kind of help that is available when caring for a child with a disability, special need or disorder.

Mental health services for children and adolescents

Framework for the Assessment of Children in Need and their Families

These are guidelines, produced by the Department of Health in 2000, to help social work professionals assess looked after children and children moving to adoption.

The National Clinical Director for Children, Young People and the Transition to Adulthood

Was appointed to oversee the NHS Commissioning Board and how services are commissioned for children. Child and adolescent mental health and emotional well-being is one of six key areas to be addressed by the framework.

Ensuring your child receives the care to which he or she is entitled

Current legislation regarding children in England and Wales promotes the provision of co-ordinated, quality health services for children. This legislation may support your case if you think your child is not receiving needed services. Copies of current legislation are available from the Department of Health.

Children's Services Plans

These are broad strategic plans designed to co-ordinate all services for vulnerable children, such as Education Development Plans, Early Years Development Plans, and Behaviour Support Plans. Co-ordination of all plans required for vulnerable children will be provided by local councils, with the full participation of NHS organisations (required by the "duty of partnership" described in the Health Act 1999).

HELPFUL RESOURCES

Organisations and information to help adopted children and adults who were adopted as children

Talk Adoption

A free, confidential national helpline for young people up to 25 years old who have a link with adoption, whether adopted person, friend or relative.
Tel: 0808 808 1234
www.afteradoption.org.uk/talkadoption-young-people

Become

A charity that promotes services for children and young people in public care, those who have left care, and those whose lives continue to be affected by their care experiences. Provides training, support and a coaching programme for young people.
15 White Lion Street
London N1 9PG
Freephone: 0800 023 2033
www.becomecharity.org.uk

To contact birth parents/relatives

Adoption Contact Register for England and Wales

Adoptions Section Room C202
The General Register Office
Adoptions Section
Trafalgar Road
Southport
Merseyside PR8 2HH
Tel: 0300 123 1837
www.gov.uk/adoption-records

Adoption Contact Register for Scotland
Birthlink
21 Castle Street
Edinburgh EH2 3DN
Tel: 0131 225 6441
www.birthlink.org.uk

General Register Office for Northern Ireland
NISRA
Colby House
Stranmillis Court
Belfast BT9 5RR
Tel: 0300 200 7890
www.nidirect.gov.uk/gro

General and health resources for children and young adults

Citizens Advice Bureau Advice Guide
Online help from Citizens Advice on young people and various health matters, including sexual health, drugs and alcohol, contraception, medical treatment, self-harm, and much more. www.adviceguide.org.uk

Child and Adolescent Mental Health
The CAMH website provides a free and comprehensive source of information for young people, parents and professionals about a range of mental health difficulties and disorders that may be encountered during childhood and adolescence.
www.camh.org.uk

National Careers Service
Set up after the closure of the Connexions service in 2012, this website provides advice and information on careers and higher/further education for young people.
www.nationalcareersservice.direct.gov.uk

Mind
Provides advice and support to empower anyone experiencing a mental health problem. Mind also campaigns to improve services, raise awareness and promote understanding of mental health issues.
15–19 Broadway
Stratford
London E15 4BQ
www.mind.org.uk

Scottish Health on the Web (SHOW)
Provided by the NHS in Scotland, this site provides general health information, contact details of all NHS Trusts, and links to other websites.
www.scot.nhs.uk/

UK Youth
A leading national youth development charity which develops, promotes and delivers a range of innovative education programmes in partnership with a national network of organisations. They aim to enable young people to raise their aspirations, realise their potential and have their achievements recognised.
483 Liverpool Road
London N7 8PG
Tel: 020 3137 3810
Email: info@ukyouth.org
www.ukyouth.org

YoungMinds
The UK's leading charity committed to improving the emotional wellbeing and mental health of children and young people and empowering their parents and carers. YoungMinds parents' helpline:
Tel: 0808 802 5544
www.youngminds.org.uk

For adoptive parents

5

In this section

→ Identify and focus on your particular needs as adoptive parents

→ Consider some of the most common emotions adoptive parents and couples encounter and better understand why these feelings occur

→ Understand the importance of taking care of yourself and your relationship (if you are a couple) through and beyond the adoption process

→ Find the resources, organisations and services that can help you help yourself through the various emotions of the adoption experience, including during times of stress

Introduction

By its very nature, adoption is a process that has its ups and downs. The experience of having a child, by birth or adoption, is always a journey into the unknown – none of us knows if our expected child will have any physical or emotional difficulties. Yet, because adoption is a process of bringing a child into your home and family, you can be fairly certain you will encounter some degree of difficulty at some point along the way.

Indeed, the transition to parenthood for most couples represents a fundamental shift in their couple relationship, as both partners begin the journey of welcoming and accommodating to a new family member.

The first step is to accept that adopting a child is different from giving birth to a child. You will have to adjust your preconceptions and your expectations about parenthood and having children. It is important to remember that adopted children, regardless of age, will be affected (to varying degrees) by the separation from their birth parents and some may also have experienced disturbance beyond the trauma of the adoption itself. As a result, these children may at times be troubled by periods of deep insecurity, which will likely impact their relationship with you and your relationship with each other (if you are a couple). In view of this, it is important that you understand and embrace the complexities of welcoming an adopted child or children into your life, so that you can be better prepared to meet the challenges alongside the inevitable rewards.

(Material in this chapter has been provided by Damian McCann, D.Psy. Syst. Head of Learning and Development, Couple Psychoanalytic Psychotherapist and Clinical Lecturer, at Tavistock Relationships. For more information on Tavistock Relationships and the services they offer, visit: www.tavistockrelationships.org.)

Adoptive parents' needs are important too

Adoption focuses on meeting the needs of a child. But this does not mean we should ignore the needs of adoptive parents. After all, if you do not look after your own physical and emotional needs, you won't be able to provide much help to your child. If you are a couple, attending to your own relationship is part of the glue that holds adoptive placements together and provides nurture for all concerned.

Yet, every adoption is an individual event and everyone responds differently to it. So while we can't predict every emotional response you may have throughout your adoption – and thus offer "answers" to every difficulty – we can describe some general feelings that most adopters experience and offer some general advice. We will also focus on the parental couple relationship of adopters, since how well things are going in your relationship will have a major bearing on the placement's strength and its ability to overcome the challenges adopted children may bring.

Although it is difficult to "avoid" having certain experiences and feelings throughout adoption, just being aware of the feelings you might have can often help you get through particular experiences more easily.

If you have not yet adopted, or only recently adopted, it may help for you to be prepared for some for the feelings you may experience that are particular to adopting a child. If you have already adopted, perhaps reading about some of the most common emotions adoptive parents face will reassure you that others have similar feelings. This can bolster your confidence as an adoptive parent.

Feelings adoptive parents commonly encounter throughout the adoption experience

"Instant" parenthood

Despite the months (perhaps years) of planning for your adopted child, it is difficult to be fully prepared for the child's arrival in your home. You can easily prepare for your child's physical needs. But being ready for your and your child's emotional responses (no matter what age child you have adopted) is altogether different. This is particularly true for individuals or couples who have not parented a child before – either born to them, fostered or adopted. The first few months after the placement can be a time of joy, but may also bring feelings of guilt, depression, perhaps even panic. The question, 'Have we done the right thing?', might enter your head more than a few times after the child is first placed with you or after the adoption goes through.

It is important, at this stage, to remember that you are a new parent, or new to parenting this child, and have taken on an immense challenge. You may find it helpful to share your true feelings with others – especially with other adoptive parents. It will also be important to give yourself "respite" time away from your child in order to "rest and recoup" from the stresses of parenting an adopted child.

Some prospective adopters can suffer symptoms of depression in the early placement period and at significant other times after an adoption. It can typically appear about a month after placement, shares some characteristics with post-natal depression, and both mothers and fathers can be affected by it. The NHS provides more information at: www.nhs.uk/Livewell/adoption-and-fostering/Documents/Adoption%20UK%20Factsheet%2014%20-%20Post-adoption%20depression%20June%202013.pdf.

HELPFUL RESOURCES

Adoption UK forums

Adoption UK members have access to an online community that includes a range of forums and messageboards where members can post questions about adoption and receive answers from others who can provide useful information based on their own experiences. Adoption UK's helplines can also provide advice (see Appendix 2).

"Sharing" your child

When your child is finally placed with you, it is common to want to immerse the child in your family life – in a sense, to make the child "your own". It can be difficult, at this time, to continually remind yourself that your child is the focus of the adoption process and that you might still have some experiences (such as visits with foster carers and/or birth parents) that you may not enjoy, but which may be in the best interests of your child. It can be painful, for example, to see your newly adopted child run to his or her former foster carers' arms for comfort, or to feel your child reject you in favour of other people he or she has known previously. Moreover, children who have attachment difficulties (see Section 4) are experts at manipulating other adults to their own advantage, while rejecting you in the process. When your child is first placed with you, you may feel surprised, confused and frustrated by such experiences.

Attachment

Although adopted children are unique, the fact that they have all been through a complicated start in life will inevitably affect them in different ways. Some adopted children may be very defended and show little or no vulnerability; it is as if they have no need of you and reject your attempts to get close. Others may be overwhelmingly demanding and clingy and you or your partner may at times feel overpowered by the level of need. For the success of the placement, it is important to understand that this is a phase that has to be weathered and that, like a number of challenges associated with adoption, it will pass. The consistency of the care you offer goes a long way to reassure your child that you are there for them and that you are not going to leave them, even if they wittingly or unwittingly upset you or test you to the limit.

During these times, it is important to seek support from others – social workers, counsellors, mental health professionals, adoption support organisations, and other adoptive parents. It is also imperative to acknowledge your own feelings about being an adoptive parent and to remember that, as adoptive parents, we may not have begun our relationship with our children with immediate "love". We may have felt

HELPFUL BOOKS

Books about attachment difficulties and parenting affected children (see also Section 4)

Attachment Handbook for Foster Care and Adoption
by Gillian Schofield and Mary Beek (2nd edition), CoramBAAF, 2018

Promoting Attachment and Resilience: A guide for foster carers and adopters on using the Secure Base Model
by Gillian Schofield and Mary Beek, BAAF, 2014

Attachment, Trauma and Resilience: Therapeutic caring for children
by Kate and Brian Cairns, CoramBAAF, 2016

Attachment Theory, Child Maltreatment and Family Support: A practice and assessment model
by David Howe *et al*, Macmillan, 1999

Building the Bonds of Attachment
by Daniel A. Hughes, Jason Aronson Inc, 2006

First Steps in Parenting the Child Who Hurts: Tiddlers & Toddlers
by Caroline Archer, Jessica Kingsley Publishers, 1999

Next Steps in Parenting the Child Who Hurts: Tykes & Teens
by Caroline Archer, Jessica Kingsley Publishers, 1999

A list of books of interest to families living with, and professionals working with, children with attachment and behavioural difficulties is available from Adoption UK (see Appendix 2).

sympathy and care for the child, initially, but in some cases, true love – the ability to love the child when the child pushes rejection right at you – may take years to develop.

Remember, also, that many adoptive parents don't have the benefit of a gestation period or a "bonding time" with a young infant. Parents of children adopted after the age of two-and-a-half to three years are presented with a walking, talking individual with his or her own personality, and with the complex effects of early neglect and/or trauma. Consequently, it will take time for you to develop a deep bond with your child, just as your child will take time to attach to you.

Parenting isn't always easy!

As rewarding as it is for parents to see their children grow and develop, inevitably there will be times when parents feel under pressure or even under attack. How you approach and tackle these challenges with your adopted child will go a long way in helping your child manage

HELPFUL RESOURCES

Training and information for parents

Parenting our children
Devised by Adoption UK and provided by PAC-UK through local authorities. This course is designed specifically to help adoptive parents gain insight into their children and to help them in their challenging role. Contact Adoption UK for more information (see Appendix 2).

Enhancing Adoptive Parenting: A parenting programme for use with new adopters of challenging children by Alan Rushton and Helen Upright, BAAF, 2012
This parenting manual is written for adoption support workers and intended to make practical and relevant advice available to struggling adopters. The programme aims to support the stability of the adoptive placement, enhance parenting skills and understanding, and improve relationships.

Managing Difficult Behaviour by Clare Pallett *et al* with Eileen Fursland, 2nd edition, CoramBAAF, 2015.
A unique handbook that provides foster carers and adopters with new skills to help them improve a child's behaviour. Full of useful tips, case examples and exercises.

Various training for adoptive parents is provided by a number of organisations, including CoramBAAF, Adoption UK, PAC-UK and Family Futures.

their own internal conflicts that are often manifested in emotional and behavioural outbursts. Some adopted children attempt to cope with their own difficulties by "splitting" their parents, and although parents may consciously or unconsciously play out the good cop/bad cop model of parenting, it is important to understand that in the long term it is unhelpful for the child or adolescent to have one parent who is "all good" and one who is "all bad". To some extent, your style of parenting develops from your own experiences of being parented and may well affect how you individually and together (if you are a couple) approach the parenting task. Few couples articulate or agree a model of parenting beforehand and many find themselves struggling when the pressures and conflicts begin to arise. Some parents find themselves at loggerheads and others may even be surprised or shocked at their partner's responses to an aspect of their adopted child's behaviour. Being able to think about this, alongside other differences and difficulties that may arise, is vital for you to retain your parental authority and capacity to contain your child's feelings and behaviour.

HELPFUL BOOKS

Related by Adoption: A handbook for grandparents and other relatives (3rd edition) by Hedi Argent, BAAF, 2014. This is a very useful short book on adoption written for family members on the useful role which they can play.

'Let me explain about adoption…'

A while after having a child placed, many parents develop an understanding of their child and learn how to respond to his or her various behaviours. However, problems often arise when trying to help the "outside" world understand their child and their child's needs. Daily life may then become a series of stressful events, when activities, such as dealing with schools, grandparents, even after-school swimming lessons, become difficult because the people involved don't understand your child. You may hesitate to discuss adoption with these people, because you don't want to appear to make "excuses" for your child. Often, however, open communication is the best policy. The general public usually is unaware of the effects of early trauma on children. Explaining these effects and "educating" others in how best to respond to your child will not only help your child now, but will also help others respond more positively to your child in the future.

Looking to the future, but acknowledging the past

The fact that your child is adopted and that he or she has had experiences not shared with you is something you can never change. Often, adoptive parents may feel reluctant to talk with their child about the past. You may even feel uncomfortable being open about your child's adoption with those around you. Especially in the first few months after your child is placed with you, it is tempting to try to forget your child's past entirely in order to focus on your future together.

However, in keeping your child's needs at the centre of your thinking, it is important to be aware of signals from your child that he or she needs to talk about and affirm his or her past. The details you choose to discuss with your child and the timing of these discussions depends solely on your child's age and ability to understand certain concepts. After your child has been with you for some time and your attachment deepens, it will become easier to discuss the past. As you focus on your child's needs, you will soon find the right balance of acknowledging, in a healthy way, the facts of your child's adoption and past history. And, as your child's attachment to you becomes more secure, you will become more comfortable with the issue of contact with birth family members.

HELPFUL ORGANISATIONS

General organisations that provide help for parents

Increasingly, local authority and voluntary agencies have adoption support specialists dedicated to providing services for adoptive families. It is worth checking what is available from the agency from which you adopted your child, the agency that prepared you to adopt, the local authority where you now live, and any specialist agencies. Below are several organisations that can provide such support.

Adoption UK

A parent-to-parent network of over 1,400 members, including established and potential adoptive families. It welcomes enquiries from prospective adopters, offers support groups UK-wide, publishes leaflets and a monthly magazine written by and for adopters. It has a members' online message board.
Units 11 and 12, Vantage Business Park
Bloxham Road
Banbury OX16 9UX
Tel: 01295 752 240
Email: admin@adoptionuk.org
www.adoptionuk.org

Family Futures

Provides a range of seminars and training for parents, carers and social workers.
3 & 4 Floral Place
7–9 Northampton Grove
London N1 2PL
Tel: 020 7354 4161
Email: contact@familyfutures.co.uk
www.familyfutures.co.uk

Coram Family and Childcare

Works to support parents in bringing up children and promoting family wellbeing. Provides 'Parent Champions' befriending programme.
Coram Campus
41 Brunswick Square
London WC1N 1AZ
Tel: 020 7239 7535
email: info@familyandchildcaretrust.org
www.familyandchildcaretrust.org

Fostering Network

Offers advice and information and books and leaflets on fostering. Also publishes the quarterly magazine *Foster Care*.
87 Blackfriars Road
London SE1 8HA
Tel: 020 7620 6400
www.thefosteringetwork.org.uk

New Family Social

The UK charity for lesbian, gay, bisexual and transgender adopters, foster carers and their children. NFS provides opportunities to get advice and encouragement, and is a safe space for parents to share support and for children to gain the confidence of knowing other adopted children with LGBT parents.
Harvey's Barn
Park End, Swaffham
Bulbeck CB25 0NA
Tel: 0843 289 9457
www.newfamilysocial.org.uk

Centre for Adoption Support and Education

Provides support for families who adopt. The centre offers workshops for parents and professionals, activities for children, private consultations for parents, and opportunities to meet other adopters.
The Centre
162 Pennywell Road
Easton
Bristol BS5 0TX
Tel: 0117 955 8826
Email: info@adoptionsupportcentre.org
www.adoptionsupportcentre.org

Family Lives
A confidential helpline providing
information and support to parents.
Helpline: 0808 800 2222
www.familylives.org.uk

**Positive Parenting Publications and
Programmes**
Provides information, resources and training
for parents and those who support them.
Garth House
Leon Avenue
Cardiff CF15 7RG
Tel: 02920 810800
www.careforthefamily.org.uk

YoungMinds Parents' Information Service
A telephone service provided by
YoungMinds (see Section 4) that gives
information and advice to anyone with
concerns about the mental health of a child.
Tel: 0808 802 5544
www.youngminds.org.uk/for_parents

In short, it's important to live life "normally", while becoming aware of how your child expresses his or her need to affirm the past. "Drip feed" information to your child, bit by bit – you'll soon become familiar with signs that your child needs to talk about the past.

Give your child small portions of information at opportune moments – often, the casual moments are the most effective – in the car, on the way home from school, for example. It doesn't have to be a long, "prepared" discussion. Just affirming the past in a matter-of-fact way will help your child to incorporate his or her story into their life, and develop a healthy self-image and sense of self.

A question of guilt and anger

Parenting a child who has attachment difficulties is tough. At times, your anger and frustration with the child may exceed levels you never thought existed within you. You may then begin to question your abilities as a parent, feel guilty about your own anger and reactions to your child, and may feel inadequate to the task of parenting an adopted child. These feelings can be reinforced when other well-meaning people around us (grandparents, friends, social workers, spouses) do not see or understand the child's behaviours. 'Why are you so "uptight"?', they wonder. 'Why are you so strict with your child?' They don't understand your emotions, because they don't spend the same amount of time with the child as you do and they don't see that your child may have rejecting behaviours that are targeted at you – the main caregiver. These will be times of extreme frustration and anxiety for you. It will be important for you to seek the support of adoption support organisations and services.

HELPFUL BOOKS

Talking about Adoption to your Adopted Child (fifth edition) by Marjorie Morrison, BAAF, 2012
A useful guide that explains how and when to explain to your child that he or she is adopted.

Adoption Conversations: What, when and how to tell by Renée Wolfs, BAAF, 2008
Explores the questions adopted children are likely to ask, with suggestions for helpful explanations and age-appropriate answers.

More Adoption Conversations: What, when and how to tell by Renée Wolfs, BAAF, 2010
Explores the problems that adopted teenagers are likely to confront and provides suggestions for helpful solutions and achievable communication methods.

What happens when things get out of hand

Evidence is emerging of some adopted children exhibiting acts of violence towards one or both parents and possibly even towards siblings and, similarly, there are also reports of parents "losing it" with each other and with their adopted child or children. This is perhaps symptomatic of the increasing pressures within the family, suggesting that help may be needed in supporting the family in regaining control of the situation. Adoption support, including "looked after children's services", offering both individual and family therapy in times of crisis, may be helpful in ensuring that the situation doesn't get out of control. Selwyn *et al* (*Beyond the Adoption Order,* BAAF, 2015) found that violence towards parents constituted the primary reason for adopted children having to leave their placements. It appears that in heterosexual couple placements, mothers were found to bear the brunt of the violence whilst fathers frequently struggled to modulate their own feelings of outrage towards their child's violent behaviour. Some of these fathers withdrew and avoided dealing with the conflict, whilst others attempted to impose strict disciplinary boundaries. When this fails to settle or resolve the situation, couples may find themselves attacking their own relationship or responding to their adopted child in an aggressive and rejecting matter – a feeling that the only choice is between sacrificing the child to save the marriage or sacrificing the marriage to save the child. Clearly these situations speak to a desperation that calls for help and couples and parents really shouldn't ignore this need.

Attending to the importance of your couple relationship

Keeping your couple relationship in focus

Taking care of the couple relationship of adoptive parents is vital, especially since it fundamentally contributes to the stability of the family as a whole, prevents adoption breakdown and ultimately supports the future wellbeing and development of the adopted child. However (as with all parents), given that partners often, in the context of parenthood, direct their focus away from their own relationship and onto their child or children, the time and effort they devote to each other is thus diminished. It is worth noting that studies indicate a decline in relationship satisfaction as well as a significant increase in couple conflict during the first year of parenthood (Shapiro *et al*, 'The baby and the marriage', *Journal of Family Psyhology*, 2000). For many, this conflict comes as something of a surprise, since couples often imagine a perfect transition. And although conflict in most couple relationships is to be expected, fights which are frequent, intense and which cannot be resolved inevitably impact and have a detrimental effect not only on your couple relationship but also on your child or children.

The dangers of only putting your best foot forward

Throughout the adoption process, couples often make considerable effort to promote only the positive aspects of their relationship, fearing that if they show any doubt or dissent they will not be considered appropriate to adopt. Yet, for many adoptive couples, the decision to adopt is far from straightforward. For instance, a number of couples will, through infertility, experience the loss of giving birth to their own child, a situation that may provoke a crisis in the relationship as you individually and together begin the process of mourning this loss. For some, the decision to adopt will represent a natural moving on, whilst for others it may signal an attempt to sidestep the mourning process associated with infertility. However, when the adopted child starts behaving in ways that feel contrary to your expectations, you may find yourself once again in touch with reminders that this is not your biological child, an awareness that may unsettle and disturb. Similarly, adopted children who in adolescence seek to repair their early broken attachments through a premature desire to close the gap by having a child of their own, will likely act as a further reminder of the difficulty you experienced with infertility.

For others, i.e. couples who make a conscious decision not to have children of their own, same-sex couples who eschew donor insemination or surrogacy and those who, for whatever reason, find themselves raising an adopted child, you may also be confronted with hidden challenges that unsettle your couple relationship. Although you may recognise that adopted children come with complicated histories, the child's own abandonment anxieties may result in them rejecting you as their parents, which, in turn, may create anxieties as you begin to question your decision to adopt. For some couples, this can spark a process of self-doubt where one of the partners may hold rigidly to hope and the other to despair. These, along with other unexpected challenges, may well pose a challenge to your relationship or indeed the placement itself and could indicate a need for adoption support and possibly even couple therapy to help you work through the immediate crisis alongside any underlying issues that may not have been fully addressed during the adoption process.

Timing is everything

Although the adoption process from assessment through to matching may take many months, the point at which the child enters your life may also throw up complex thoughts and feelings. Some couples feel that they have waited too long, whilst others feel the pressure to adopt and are not quite ready when the child arrives. On occasions, ambivalent feelings in one or both partners may surface and this can complicate the otherwise joyful experience of welcoming the child or children into your life. The question as to whether you have done the right thing may also come to mind and leave you feeling alone and exposed.

It is important to try to find time for each other, as well as talking to your family and friends when needed. For couples who welcome an adopted child into an already existing family, integrating that child and managing the impact of this on your other children may provide additional challenges that may also warrant extra support. The point of this handbook is to remind you that you are not alone and that asking for help is not a sign of weakness or failure.

Adoption support

In 2013, the Government published the Adoption Passport (updated in 2017), a short guide which sets out the support services adopters can expect from local authorities. The Passport is available on the First4Adoption website (www.first4adoption.org.uk) and is shown in Appendix 5.

The Adoption Support Services Regulations 2005, the Adoption Guidance 2011, the National Minimum Standards 2011 and the Practice Guidance on Assessing the Support Needs of Adoptive Families all address support issues.

Adoption Guidance states that:

'The provision of a range of adoption support services is a crucial element of the statutory framework introduced by the [Adoption and Children] Act

[2002]. This is based on the recognition that adopted children and their families are likely to have a range of additional needs.' Guidance 9.1.

Children and adults affected by adoption receive an assessment of their adoption support needs from their agency. Service users confirm that the adoption support service provided either met or is meeting their assessed needs. When deciding whether to provide a service, or which service to provide, the agency has regard to the assessed needs for adoption support services, listens to the service user's wishes and feelings and considers their welfare and safety (NMS 15).

There is no need for adoptive parents, couples and children to struggle on their own when services exist to shore up the placement when the going gets tough, or indeed falls outside the bounds of what feels manageable.

Adoption Support Fund

Adopters in England can access the Adoption Support Fund (ASF), which was established by the Government to help families access funds for therapeutic support.

The ASF is available for children living in England up to and including the age of 21 (or 25 with an Education Health and Care Plan), who:

- are adopted and were previously in local authority care in England, Wales, Scotland or Northern Ireland;
- are adopted from overseas;
- are subject to a special guardianship order.

  To access the ASF, your family's adoption support needs will have to be assessed by the local authority. The ASF will provide money for a range of therapeutic services if it is shown that they can help achieve one of the following outcomes for you and your child:

- improved relationships with friends, family members, teachers and school staff;
- improved engagement with learning;
- improved emotional regulation and behaviour management;
- improved confidence and ability to enjoy a positive family life and social relationships.

  For more information, visit www.adoptionsupportfund.co.uk/.

HELPFUL RESOURCES

The Adopter's Handbook on Therapy: Getting the best for your child
by Eileen Fursland, CoramBAAF, 2016

This practical guide offers clear and informative summaries of the different therapies and therapeutic support programmes that are available, as well as support groups and other resources for adoptive parents. Personal accounts from adopters who have benefited from these approaches help readers understand how therapy could help their child.

Other routes to support

You could begin by visiting your GP and requesting referral to a consultant child psychologist, psychiatrist or psychotherapist. You could also consult the organisations and services listed in Section 4 as well as those in this section. In addition, local authorities and voluntary adoption agencies provide adoption support, but services available from different agencies are variable. Contact your agency to find out what they offer.

Will we be able to have adoption support services from a local authority, even if we adopted several years ago?

Yes. This is described in Section 4. You have a right to an assessment of your adoption support needs. Remember that approaching professionals at an adoption support centre, or adoption or adoption support workers (ASSAs) in your local authority will be important, especially at times of crises, as these professionals will have a good understanding of adoption and therefore could be particularly helpful.

Adoptive couple therapy

Tavistock Relationships (www.tavistockrelationships.org/) offers a specialist adoptive couples therapy service that also addresses parental concerns. Couples and parents are able to book online and, following an initial consultation, may be offered couples therapy, parenting work or couples group therapy. Although this specialist service is based in London, there is an online option enabling adoptive couples and parents across the country to access this service.

About disruption

"Disruption" is a term commonly used by social workers to describe an adoption (or foster placement) that does not work out.

Most adoption placements succeed rather than fail. But some placements do disrupt (i.e. break down), for many reasons: for instance, if the child and adoptive parents are unable to bond or attach to each other; if the child has difficulties for which the adoptive parents were not adequately prepared; or if there is not adequate adoption support for the family. Local authorities will always try to find a way to help you or the child before taking the difficult decision to bring the child back to foster care.

Needless to say, disrupted adoptions bring immense grief, guilt and anger to both the adoptive parents and for the child. Some local authorities and adoption agencies provide a "disruption meeting". This meeting will include the adopters, all involved social workers, the current carers for the child, possibly the birth parents. It is independently chaired. It considers the adoptive parents' histories up to the match, how the match came to be made and what happened during the placement and how it ended. The aim is to inform ongoing work with and planning for the child and to help everyone involved to reflect on, understand and learn from what happened.

Helping yourself and helping your child

No two adoptions are the same. You may meet other adoptive families whose experiences will be different from yours.

Hundreds of children in the UK need adoptive families. These children are in need of families in which they can grow and mature within a loving and secure environment. But adoption certainly is not an "easy" road to travel for these children or for their adoptive parents, and it takes a certain type of parent to make the personal sacrifices required of adopters.

As we stated previously, the purpose of this guide is to help you to help yourself on your journey through adoption. No matter what stage you're at in the process – for example, just considering adoption, waiting to be matched with a child, or seeking post-adoption help many years after your child's placement – there are a rapidly increasing number of services and resources that can help you.

Every year around 3,000–5,000 children in the UK are legally adopted. New families are formed. The interplay of personalities and complex issues faced by both the child and the adults creates unique and varied experiences for the adoptive family. You can be certain, therefore, that you may meet other adoptive families whose experiences might be similar to yours, but rarely exactly the same. Because no two adoptions are the same, you also may encounter services (for example, school and health services) that have little experience of the problems you face with your adopted child. Increased publicity and media attention about adoption increases the general public's understanding of these issues. Yet, despite such publicity and the increasing focus on post-adoption services, you are likely to encounter a significant lack of knowledge and/or understanding about adoption within the general public.

So, what can you do to help yourself?

Firstly, use this guide to communicate with others: with your child's teachers, doctors, babysitter or childminder, birth family members, your own family members, and any other people your child may interact with frequently. Use the guide to inform them about certain issues and/or to find more specific information about these issues.

Secondly, think laterally and creatively! If you and your child are facing specific problems, be aware that solutions to the problem may not always be obvious or straightforward. And remember that there may be several interacting issues that underline one problem. If, for example, your eight-year-old son still has significant problems with soiling and wetting (even though he has been with you for four years), you may have several "causes" to consider: insecurity, anxiety, physical problems and attachment issues, to name a few. But thinking "laterally", you may also have to consider that your son may never have had any formal toilet training, unlike most toddlers. This is a consideration that, understandably, may never have crossed your mind while you were going through the adoption process four years earlier.

As an adoptive parent, you will be challenged, almost daily, to come up with creative strategies to address your child's needs. Use this guide as a starting point for information, and remember that you may have to tailor some of the information and advice in order to suit your child's particular needs.

Parenting children, in general, is not an easy task. Being an adoptive parent adds its own unique challenges. But, by sharing information in a direct, factual and creative manner, adoptive parents can reduce the stress of unexpected problems, address issues in a calm, practical and informed manner, and look forward to a successful and rewarding experience.

Help us to help you! Because the adoption process and associated services are developing and changing so rapidly, this guide may not provide all the answers you may need. Inevitably, you may come across organisations, publications or services that are not listed here. If so, please inform us.

By sharing information in a direct, factual and creative manner, adoptive parents can reduce the stress of unexpected problems, address issues in a calm, practical and informed manner, and look forward to a successful and rewarding experience for their children and for themselves.

Appendices

Appendix 1:
Books, journals and magazines

Appendix 2:
Organisations, government agencies, websites

Appendix 3:
Extracts from National Minimum Standards for Adoption (2011) applicable to the provision of adoption services

Appendix 4:
The Adoption Passport

Appendix 1:
Books, journals and magazines

The publications listed here are a compilation of most of the publications listed within this handbook, and are only a sample of the information available. See www.corambaaf.org.uk for more books published by BAAF, now CoramBAAF.

Books for prospective adopters/ adoptive parents

Guides to adoptive parenting

Adopted Children Speaking by Caroline Thomas and Verna Beckford, BAAF, 1999. Provides moving and poignant testimonies which offer revealing insights into children's feelings about adoption. Available as a pdf.

Adopting a Child by Jenifer Lord, CoramBAAF, 2016 (11th edition). This guide describes what adoption means and how to go about it, including procedures and practices, legal requirements and the costs involved.

Adoption Conversations: What, when and how to tell, by Renée Wolfs, BAAF, 2008. Explores the questions adopted children are likely to ask, with suggestions for helpful explanations and age-appropriate answers.

Attachment, Trauma and Resilience, by Kate and Brian Cairns, CoramBAAF, 2016. In this remarkable book, Kate and Brian Cairns draw upon their personal and professional experience to offer an insight into the realities of family life with children who have lived through overwhelming stress. Vividly described scenarios show how they responded to the children's powerful feelings and difficult behaviours following their experiences of attachment difficulties, loss, abuse and trauma.

Brain-Based Parenting: The Neuroscience of Caregiving for Healthy Attachment, Daniel A Hughes and Jonathan Baylin, WW Norton, 2012. In this ground-breaking exploration of the brain mechanisms behind healthy caregiving, attachment specialist Daniel A Hughes and veteran clinical psychologist Jonathan Baylin guide readers through the intricate web of neuronal processes, hormones, and chemicals that drive – and sometimes thwart – our caregiving impulses, uncovering the mysteries of the parental brain.

Digital Life Story Work by Simon P Hammond and Neil J Cooper, BAAF, 2012. A practical guide which looks at how to use computers, smartphones and camcorders with older children and adolescents in fun and creative life story work projects.

Facing up to Facebook by Eileen Fursland, BAAF, 2013. The use of Facebook and other social networking websites has already had an impact on many adoptive families and has the potential to affect many more. Increasingly, young people are using social networking websites to trace and contact their birth parents or other birth relatives. Birth relatives are using the internet to trace their children. Facing up to Facebook provides a considerable amount of information, raises important questions and offers essential advice.

First Steps in Parenting the Child Who Hurts: Tiddlers and toddlers by Caroline Archer, Jessica Kingsley, 1999. Discusses the attachment and developmental issues that arise when even the youngest child is in your care.

Flying Solo by Julia Wise, BAAF, 2007. Tells Julia Wise's story of adopting solo. It's a very personal story, but one that will resonate loudly with single adopters everywhere. Julia offers a realistic look at the joys and pitfalls of adopting on her own and the impact of her decision on herself, her family and close friends. Part of

CoramBAAF's series of personal narratives that deal with a wide range of adoption scenarios.

Life Story Work by Tony Ryan and Rodger Walker, CoramBAAF, 2016 (4th edn). A popular guide that provides insight, ideas and exercises to use for life story work.

More Adoption Conversations: What, when and how to tell, by Renée Wolfs, BAAF, 2010. Explores the problems that adopted teenagers are likely to confront and provides suggestions for helpful solutions and achievable communication methods.

Next Steps in Parenting the Child Who Hurts: Tykes and teens by Caroline Archer, Jessica Kingsley, 1999. This book follows on logically from the First Steps book and continues into the challenging journey through childhood and into adolescence.

Our Adoption Journey by Jayne Lilley, CoramBAAF, 2016. This is the true story of Jayne, Dan, their son Charlie, and their adoption of Jessie, a baby girl. Told by Jayne, this moving memoir follows the joyful highs and heartbreaking lows of the journey that led them to their new adopted daughter.

One of the Family: A handbook for kinship carers by Hedi Argent, BAAF, 2005. This handbook aims to give families and friends who may become kinship carers information about the choices they can make, the assessment process, legal framework and the support they can expect.

Parenting Matters: A series of short informative books that offer expert information on some health-related conditions often associated with looked after and adopted children, combined with personal accounts from parents and carers who have cared for children affected by these conditions. Titles cover emotional and behavioural difficulties, parental substance misuse, attention deficit hyperactivity disorder, dyslexia, mental health issues, autism spectrum disorder, developmental delay, genetic disorders, sexual abuse, domestic abuse, and trauma.

The Pink Guide to Adoption for Lesbians and Gay Men (2nd edn) by Nicola Hill, BAAF, 2012. An essential step-by-step guide to the adoption process for lesbians and gay men considering adoption, which also includes interviews with and stories from several lesbians and gay men at various stages of the adoption process.

Preparing to Adopt: A training pack for preparation groups by Eileen Fursland, CoramBAAF, 2014 (3rd edn). A training pack, consisting of a trainer's guide, an applicant's workbook and a video, designed to prepare prospective adopters for all the aspects of the adoption process.

Proud Parents by Nicola Hill, BAAF, 2013. A collection of stories of lesbians and gay men who have adopted or fostered children, which looks at their motivations, their response to the assessment process, what it was like when the child moved in, and what life is like as a family.

Related by Adoption: A handbook for grandparents and other relatives by Hedi Argent with a contribution from Kate Cairns, CoramBAAF, 2014 (3rd edition). This brief and sensitively written handbook aims to give grandparents-to-be and other relatives information about adoption today and how the wider family can support building a family through adoption.

Talking about Adoption to your Adopted Child by Marjorie Morrison, BAAF, 2012 (4th edition). A useful guide that advises how and when to explain to your child that he or she is adopted.

The Great Behaviour Breakdown by B Bryan Post, Post Publishing, 2009. Step-by-step guidance and insight on understanding the causes, and impactful methods to help deal with some of the most serious, problematic and challenging behaviours.

Legal and financial issues

Adoption Now: Law, regulations, guidance and standards by Fergus Smith and Roy Stewart with Alexandra Conroy Harris, BAAF, 2013 (3rd edition). A handy pocket book, covering all essential information on the law, regulations, guidance and standards relating to adoption.

Child Care Law: A summary of the law in England and Wales by Deborah Cullen and Alexandra Conroy Harris, BAAF, 2014. Quick-reference guide to the law (in England and Wales) regarding the care of children.

Child Care Law: Scotland by Alexandra Plumtree, BAAF, 2014. Quick-reference guide to the law (in Scotland) regarding the care of children.

Child Care Law: Northern Ireland by Michael Long, CoramBAAF, 2018 (2nd edition). Quick-reference guide to the law (in Northern Ireland) regarding the care of children.

Effective Adoption Panels (7th edn) by Jenifer Lord and Deborah Cullen, CoramBAAF, 2016. Provides guidance on regulations, process and good practice in adoption and permanence panels.

Schooling

The Adopter's Handbook on Education, by Eileen Fursland, CoramBAAF, 2018 Provides straightforward, practical information on how parents can help to ensure their adopted child gets the most out of their education, with advice on working with school staff, support and terminology.

Attachment, Developmental Trauma and Executive Functioning Difficulties in the School Setting, by Marion Allen, Family Futures, 2008. Provides strategies and interventions to manage behaviour and establish an environment which will enable children to achieve their personal and academic potential.

Attachment in the Classroom: The links between children's early experience, emotional wellbeing and performance in school, by Heather Geddes, Worth Publishing, 2006. Explores the significance of the relationship between the pupil, the teacher and the learning task, linking it to emotional development, behaviour and attachment experiences.

Inside I'm Hurting: Practical strategies for supporting children with attachment difficulties in schools, by Louise Michelle Bombèr, Worth Publishing, 2007. Provides educational professionals with a much needed classroom handbook of strategies, practical tools and the confidence for supporting children (who have experienced trauma) from an attachment perspective.

Learn the Child: Helping looked after children to learn by Kate Cairns and Chris Stanway, BAAF, 2013 (2nd edition). A resource pack, consisting of a book and CD ROM, which looks at the long-term effects of trauma in childhood and how this can affect learning, with suggestions for how traumatised children can best be supported by carers and professionals.

Special Educational Needs: A guide for parents Department for Education and Skills (DfES), 2014. See Appendix 2 for contact details.

Special Needs: A guide for parents and carers of Jewish children with special educational needs Available from the Board of Deputies of British Jews, Tel: 020 7543 5400.

Supporting Children in Public Care in Schools: A resource for trainers of teachers, carers and social workers by John Holland and Catherine Randerson, Jessica Kingsley Publishers, 2005. A comprehensive training resource which provides guidance on how to support children who have faced loss as a result of significant changes in placement.

Ten Top Tips on Supporting Education by Eileen Fursland with Kate Cairns and Chris Stanway, BAAF, 2013. Aimed at social workers but also of use to adopters, this short guide looks at ten fundamental steps that can be undertaken to help adopted and looked after children thrive in education.

Physical and mental health and disability issues

The Adopters Handbook on Therapy by Eileen Fursland, CoramBAAF, 2016. Adoption offers a new start and a loving home for many children. However, for many children, putting the past behind them isn't easy – here, therapy can help. This guide offers clear and factual summaries of the different therapies and therapeutic parenting programmes that are available, as well as support groups and other resources.

Parent Participation: Improving services for disabled children, Council for Disabled Children and Contact a Family

Attachment issues

Attachment Handbook for Foster Care and Adoption by Gillian Schofield and Mary Beek, CoramBAAF, 2018. A comprehensive and authoritative textbook which provides an accessible account of core attachment concepts. Forthcoming: new edition in 2018.

Attachment, Trauma and Resilience by Kate and Brian Cairns, CoramBAAF, 2016. In this remarkable book, Kate and Brian Cairns draw upon their personal and professional experience to offer an insight into the realities of family life with children who have lived through overwhelming stress. Vividly described scenarios show how they responded to the children's powerful feelings and difficult behaviours following their experiences of attachment difficulties, loss, abuse and trauma.

Building the Bonds of Attachment by Daniel Hughes, Jason Aronson, 2006 (2nd edition). Critically acclaimed book for those who strive to assist poorly attached children, which blends attachment theory, research, and trauma theory with general principles of parenting and family therapy.

Connecting with Kids through Stories: Using narratives to facilitate attachment in adopted children, by Denise Lacher, Todd Nichols and Joanne May, Jessica Kingsley Publishers, 2011 (2nd edition). An accessible guide to family attachment narrative therapy for the parents of adopted or fostered children.

Facilitating Developmental Attachment: The road to emotional recovery and behavioural change in foster and adopted children by Daniel A. Hughes, Jason Aronson, Inc., 1997, USA. An easy-to-read book written by a leading clinical psychologist in the U.S. who specialises in helping foster and adopted children and families. The book provides an in-depth look at attachment issues in children and provides many strategies for parents.

Promoting Attachment and Resilience by Gillian Schofield and Mary Beek, BAAF, 2014. This practical guide is designed to support foster carers and adopters in offering the best possible sensitive care for troubled children who have often experienced trauma and loss, using the Secure Base Model. It provides a valuable framework and strength-based approach for making sense of fostered and adopted children's needs and behaviours and sets out the dimensions of caregiving that can support children to thrive and to fulfil their potential.

Together in Time, by Ruth and Ed Royce, BAAF, 2008. Ruth and Ed look back on their decision to adopt a boy with attachment difficulties, the fear that their family was falling apart, and their experience of music and art therapy.

Trauma, Attachment and Family Permanence: Fear can stop you loving, edited by Caroline Archer and Alan Burnell, Jessica Kingsley Publishers, 2003. Draws on the programmes offered by Family Futures to explore the challenges faced by the professional or parent who seeks to promote family permanence. Brings together a rich selection of ideas.

Understanding Attachment and Attachment Disorders: Theory, evidence and practice by Vivien Prior and Danya Glaser, Jessica Kingsley

Publishers, 2006. An examination and discussion of the scientific evidence on attachment, its influence on development, and attachment disorders.

Intercountry adoption

Children Adopted from Abroad: Key health and developmental issues, BAAF, 2004. A pamphlet aimed at intercountry adopters, which advises on possible child health problems and the screening of children adopted from overseas. Available as a pdf for CoramBAAF members.

Intercountry Adoption by Cherry Harnott, BAAF, 2010. A pamphlet which describes the intercountry adoption process, issues and implications for families involved, and basic practical guidance on procedures and rules.

A Procedural Guide to Intercountry Adoption Available from the Intercountry Adoption Centre. See Appendix 2 for contact details.

Policy and Practice Implications from the English and Romanian Adoptees (ERA) Study: Forty-five key questions by Michael Rutter *et al*, BAAF, 2009. Focuses on the policy and practice implications of this internationally known study, which answers 45 key questions most often posed by practitioners and policy makers.

Search and reunion

Searching Questions: Identity, origins and adoption by Julia Feast and Terry Philpot, BAAF, 2003 (book and DVD). Highlights the issues involved in searching and reunion. Designed for training, discussion groups or individuals who have been affected by these subjects.

Other books/articles

A Child's Journey through Placement by Vera Fahlberg, BAAF, 1994. Clear, informative and insightful and full of practical ideas and case examples, this essential reference book contains the knowledge base and skills for understanding and working with children and their families.

Children Exposed to Parental Substance Misuse edited by Rena Phillips, BAAF, 2004. This anthology looks at the effects on children of drugs, alcohol and other substances misused by parents, especially mothers, during pregnancy. Contains invaluable tools, suggestions and resources.

The Colours in Me: Writing and poetry by adopted children and young people edited by Perlita Harris, BAAF, 2008. Over 80 contributors, ranging from four to 20 years of age, tell it like it is, revealing what it feels like and what it means to be adopted.

Coming Home to Self: Healing the primal wound by Nancy Newton Verrier, BAAF, 2010. The sequel to *The Primal Wound*, this book examines the effects of separation trauma on brain development and looks at ways of regulating emotions and healing the self.

In Search of Belonging: Reflections of transracially adopted children edited by Perlita Harris, BAAF, 2006. This is the first UK publication to give voice to child and adult transracial adoptees, bringing together poetry, artwork, memoirs and writings from over 50 transracial and transnational UK adoptees.

Mother Me: An adopted woman's journey to motherhood by Zara H Phillips, BAAF, 2008. This frank and honest account explores the far-reaching impact of adoption on the author's childhood, adolescence, relationships and self-esteem, along with a unique insight into pregnancy and motherhood from the perspective of an adopted woman.

Once Upon a Time by Joan Moore, BAAF, 2012. Provides help and resources for those undertaking direct work with children. It contains a rich compendium of stories and drama – original, adapted, popular and made up by children – that explore how using storytelling and play in direct work with children can help both parents/carers and their child to build rapport and improve their relationship.

The Primal Wound: Understanding the adopted child by Nancy Newton Verrier, BAAF, 2009.

A classic in adoption literature, in this book the author explores what she calls the "primal wound" that results when a child is separated from his or her mother, and the trauma and life-long consequences that can result.

Special and Odd by James Mulholland, BAAF, 2007. A revealing and extraordinarily witty memoir in which the author tells the story of how he met his birth mother, 29 years after being given up for adoption, and the effect this had on him and his adoptive family.

The Birth Father's Tale by Andrew Ward, BAAF, 2012. A personal account by a birth father, who describes his search for his son and illustrates how being a birth father has affected his relationships, career and attitudes.

Together or Apart? Assessing brothers and sisters for permanent placement by Jenifer Lord and Sarah Borthwick, BAAF, 2008 (2nd edn). Looks at the factors that should be considered in placing sibling groups. Forthcoming: new edition in 2018.

Books for children who have been adopted

Adoption: What it is and what it means by Shaila Shah, BAAF, 2012. A short, brightly illustrated guide to adoption for children and young people, which sets out information about the processes and procedures simply and clearly.

Chester and Daisy Move On by Angela Lidster, illustrations by Robyn Allpress, BAAF, 1995. This engaging picture book is for use with children who are moving on to adoption. It tells the story of Chester and Daisy, two little bear cubs who have to leave their parents and live with a new bear family.

Dad David, Baba Chris and Me by Ed Merchant, BAAF, 2010. This brightly illustrated book for children aged 5–10 years old tells the story of Ben's life with his adoptive gay parents and how, after teasing at school, his teacher helps the class to understand that children live in all kinds of families.

Josh and Jaz have Three Mums by Hedi Argent, BAAF, 2007. This brightly illustrated book tells the story of Josh and Jaz, five-year-old twins who have been adopted by a lesbian couple. Having to draw a family tree for school teaches their class about different family structures and diversity.

Life Story Work: What it is and what it means by Shaila Shah and Hedi Argent, BAAF, 2006. This new booklet, for children and young people who are embarking on life story work or are already doing it, explains what it is and how it is undertaken.

My Life and Me by Jean Camis, BAAF, 2001. A colourful and comprehensive life story workbook which will help children develop and record memories and recollections of their past and their birth family. With comprehensive guidelines for the adult working with the child.

Social Networking and You by Eileen Fursland, BAAF, 2013. This short, colourful booklet will help to explain to adopted children and young people the importance of being safe online, particularly in relation to adoption issues. It covers protecting your privacy, thinking carefully about who can contact you, making sure your personal details are secure, and the issues and problems around getting in contact with, or being contacted by, birth relatives.

The Most Precious Present in the World by Becky Edwards, BAAF, 2010. Taking the form of a dialogue between a little girl, Mia, and her adoptive mother, this book explores questions that might preoccupy an adopted child, including why she looks different to her adoptive parents and why her birth mother didn't want to keep her.

The Nutmeg series by Judith Foxon, illustrated by Sarah Rawlings, BAAF.

Nutmeg Gets Adopted 2001

Nutmeg Gets Cross 2002

Nutmeg Gets a Letter 2003

Nutmeg Gets a Little Help 2004

Nutmeg Gets into Trouble 2006

Nutmeg Gets a Little Sister 2007

A colourful storybook series telling the story of Nutmeg the squirrel and his brother and sister, who go to live with a new family after their birth mother realises she cannot keep them safe. The books cover the painful feelings that are likely to surface following adoption; contact; post-adoption support work; and the adopted child in education.

Oh Brother! Tom gets a new adopted brother by Claire Friday, Adoption UK, 2005. Aimed at children aged between 7–11 years, this book tells the story of Tom, a birth child, whose parents decide to adopt another child, looking at Tom's hopes, fears and expectations through the approval and matching process and once Billy joins the family.

Stories for Troubled Children by Margot Sunderland, Speechmark Publishing, 2001. Five books to help children think about their feelings and to work through issues that trouble them.

Willy and the Wobbly House a story for children who are anxious or obsessional;

A Wibble Called Biley (and a Few Honks) a story for children who have hardened their hearts or who have become bullies;

A Pea Called Mildred to help children pursue their hopes and dreams;

A Nifflenoo Called Nevermind for children who bottle up their feelings;

The Frog Who Longed for the Moon to Smile for children who yearn for someone they love.

The Teazles' Baby Bunny by Susan Bagnall, BAAF, 2008. A colourful picture book for young children aged two to four years which tells the simple story of the Teazle rabbits and their adoption of a baby bunny.

What Happens in Court? by Hedi Argent and Mary Lane, BAAF, 2004. A user-friendly guide for adopted and fostered children which will help them understand the role that a court might play in their lives.

What is Contact? by Hedi Argent, BAAF, 2004. A colourful children's guide which describes what contact or "keeping in touch" means for children who are not living with their birth family.

What is a Disability? by Hedi Argent, BAAF, 2004. This children's guide explains what disabilities are and what they can mean for those who have them, with the understanding that every child is special and children with disabilities are more special in a different way.

Where is Poppy's Panda? by David Pitcher, BAAF, 2009. This beautifully illustrated book for children aged three and above explores transition, loss and change and the importance of maintaining continuity in a child's life.

Journals and magazines

Adoption & Fostering Quarterly journal of CoramBAAF. Presents current issues in practice, policy, law and research in foster care and adoption throughout the UK. For anyone involved in foster care and adoption. Available by subscription from CoramBAAF (see Appendix 2) or through SAGE Publications.

Adoption Today Monthly magazine of Adoption UK. Directed mainly at people who have adopted or who are considering adoption. Part I of the magazine includes articles, news items, letters and book reviews about adoption. Part II of the magazine, ***Children Who Wait***; also available online at www.adoptionuk.org.uk, provides information about children currently waiting to be adopted. The magazine is free with membership in Adoption UK (see Appendix 2).

Appendix 2:
Organisations, government agencies, websites

The following list details some key organisations that could be useful. They have been checked at the time of going to press, but details can change! It's best to search online as there is a wealth of information available on the internet, although you must be careful to select those organisations which are authoritative sources.

ADDISS
(The National Attention Deficit Disorder Information and Support Service)
Provides information and resources about ADHD for parents, teachers and health professionals. Resources include publications, conferences, training and local support groups.

PO Box 340
Edgware
Middlesex HA8 9HL
Tel: 020 8952 2800
email: info@addiss.co.uk
www.addiss.co.uk

Adoption agencies
First4Adoption's website has a list of adoption agencies – see www.first4adoption.org.uk.

Adoption Contact Register for England and Wales
Tel: 0300 123 1837
www.gov.uk/adoption-records/the-adoption-contact-register

Adoption Contact Register Office for Scotland
c/o Birthlink
21 Castle Street
Edinburgh EH2 3DN
Tel: 0131 225 6441
www.birthlink.org.uk

Adoption Match
Tel: 0345 222 9015
email: mail@adoptionmatch.org.uk
www.adoptionmatch.org.uk

Scotland's Adoption Register
7 John's Place
Edinburgh EH6 7EL
Tel: 0131 526 3240
email: sar@scotlandsadoptionregister.org.uk
www.scotlandsadoptionregister.org.uk

Adoption UK
A UK-wide self-help group run by adoptive parents who offer support before, during and after adoption. Services include a helpline; a magazine that includes details of children waiting for adoption; messageboards for adopters and prospective adopters to share knowledge and support each other; and printed information about all aspects of adoption.

Units 11 and 12
Vantage Business Park
Bloxham Road
Banbury
Oxfordshire OX16 9UX
Tel: 01295 752240
www.adoptionuk.org

ACE Education Advice & ACE Education Training
Provides information about all aspects of state education and helps parents who are dealing with schools or education authorities.
72 Durnsford Road
London N11 2EJ
General advice line: 0300 011 5142
www.ace-ed.org.uk

After Adoption

Offers a wide range of services and provides information, support and advice to all those affected by adoption.

Head Office
Unit 5, Citygate
5 Blantyre Street
Manchester M15 4JJ
Tel: 0800 0568 578 (for service users)
0161 839 4932 (for professionals)
www.afteradoption.org.uk

Anna Freud Centre

A research and treatment centre for children and young people with a range of emotional, behavioural and developmental difficulties. Its website includes information about its services and summaries of research into attachment and other emotional/behavioural difficulties.

12 Maresfield Gardens
London NW3 5SU
Tel: 020 7794 2313
email: info@annafreud.org
www.annafreud.org

Association for Child and Adolescent Mental Health

An association for professionals of various disciplines who are involved with children. It arranges seminars and publishes professional journals. It does not provide an advice service.

St Saviour's House
39–41 Union Street, London SE1 1SD
Tel: 020 7403 7458
email: membership@acamh.org
www.acamh.org.uk

Association of Child Psychotherapists (ACP)

Maintains register of accredited child psychotherapists and gives details of local child psychotherapists.

CAN Mezzanine
32–36 Loman Street
London SE1 0EH

Tel: 020 7922 7751
email: admin@childpsychotherapy.org.uk
www.childpsychotherapy.org.uk

Benefit Enquiry Lines

Personal independence payment tel: 0800 917 2222
Carers Allowance tel: 0345 608 4321
Disability benefits tel: 0345 712 3456 for children; 0843 504 7193 for adults
Sickness benefits tel: 0843 504 7178

Birthlink

Offers post-adoption counselling and runs Scotland's only contact register.

21 Castle Street
Edinburgh EH2 3DN
Tel: 0131 225 6441
email: mail@birthlink.org.uk
www.birthlink.org.uk

British Association for Counselling and Psychotherapy (BACP)

Can provide details of local counsellors and psychotherapists.

BACP House
15 St John's Business Park
Lutterworth LE17 4HB
Tel: 01445 883300
Monday–Friday 9.00am–5pm (information)
email: bacp@bacp.co.uk
www.bacp.co.uk

The British Psychotherapy Foundation

The training and professional institution of psychoanalytic psychotherapists, analytical psycholoists (Jungian) and child psychotherapists.

37 Mapesbury Road
London NW2 4HJ
Tel: 020 8452 9823
www.britishpsychotherapyfoundation.org.uk

British Institute for Learning Disabilities (BILD)

Services include information about learning disabilities, resources, conferences and events. Supports research into learning disabilities.

Birmingham Research Park
97 Vincent Drive
Edgbaston
Birmingham B15 2SQ
Tel: 0121 415 6960
email: enquiries@bild.org.uk
www.bild.org.uk

Caspari Foundation

Dedicated to promoting educational therapy and therapeutic learning to help children who have emotional barriers that can impair learning. Organises lectures and events.

Finspace
225–229 Seven Sisters Road
London N4 2DA
Tel: 020 7527 5161
email: admin@caspari.org.uk
www.caspari.org.uk

The Centre for Child Mental Health

Promotes awareness of the emotional well-being and mental health of children. Disseminates research to health professionals, parents and the media through conferences and publications.

2–18 Britannia Row
London N1 8PA
Tel: 020 7354 2913
email: info@childmentalhealthcentre.org
www.childmentalhealthcentre.org

Children and Families Across Borders (CFAB)

A voluntary organisation that helps families and individuals whose lives are split between different countries.

Victoria Charity Centre
11 Belgrave Road
London SW1V 1RB
Tel: 020 7735 8941
www.cfab.org.uk

Children and Family Courts Advisory and Support Service (CAFCASS)

Looks after the interests of children involved in family proceedings. They work with children and their families and advise the courts on what they consider to be in children's best interests.

3rd Floor, 21 Bloomsbury Street
London WC1B 3HF
Tel: 0844 353 4332
email: webenquiries@cafcass.gov.uk
www.cafcass.gov.uk

Children in Scotland

Provides a national information and advice service, Enquire, for parents, professionals, children and young people who have questions about special educational needs.

Level 1, Rosebery House
Edinburgh EH12 5EZ
Tel: 0131 313 2322
email: info@childreninscotland.org.uk
www.childreninscotland.org.uk

The Children's Society

UK-wide charity which provides projects and information for children and families who are experiencing difficulties, including children at risk, disabled children, children affected by adult substance misuse, post-adoption and advocacy services, and more.

Edward Rudolf House, Margery Street
London WC1X 0JL
Tel: 0300 303 7000
email: supportercare@childrens
society.org.uk
www.childrenssociety.org.uk

Community Legal Service

A government initiative designed to ensure everyone has access to quality legal advice and information. The service can be provided by CABs, solicitors' firms and legal advice centres that have been awarded the Community Legal Service Quality mark. You can find the *Community Legal Service Directory* at your local library and online. It lists all law firms and advice centres that have the Quality Mark, and indicates whether firms offer free advice.

Tel: 0345 345 4345 for information about CLS providers or about the CLS directory. www.gov.uk/civil-legal-advice

Contact a Family

Provides information online for parents on over 2,000 rare medical conditions, including information about support groups. There is also a freephone helpline for parents seeking information regarding help for disabled children.

209–211 City Road, London EC1V 1JN
Helpline: 0808 808 3555
Monday–Friday 9.30am–5pm
Tel: 020 7608 8700
email: info@cafamily.org.uk
www.cafamily.org.uk

CoramBAAF

An independent membership organisation for professionals, foster carers and adopters, and anyone else working with or looking after children in or from care, or adults who have been affected by adoption. It is a successor organisation to the British Association for Adoption and Fostering (BAAF).

41 Brunswick Square
London WC1N 1AZ
Tel: 020 7520 0300
www.corambaaf.org.uk

Coram Children's Legal Centre

Specialises in law and policy affecting children and young people. Produces information sheets and booklets. In addition to policy and campaign work, also provides an advice and information service (free and confidential legal advice).

Tel: 01206 714 650
email: info@coramclc.org.uk
www.childrenslegalcentre.com

Coram Family and Childcare

Supports parents and offers practical help in bringing up children and promotes the well-being of families. Services include publications and conferences.

Coram Campus
41 Brunswick Square
London WC1N 1AZ
Tel: 020 7239 7535
email: info@familyandchildcaretrust.org
www.familyandchildcaretrust.org

Council for Disabled Children

Promotes collaborative work between different organisations providing services and support for children and young people with disabilities and special educational needs. Offers a range of services including consultancy, training, information, publications and conferences.

8 Wakley Street, London EC1V 7QE
Tel: 020 7843 1900
email: cdc@ncb.org.uk
www.councilfordisabledchildren.org.uk

The Court Service

www.justice.gov.uk

Department for Education (DfE)

Provides information for parents about all aspects of education and schools. The DfE website provides information about SEN. Contact the DfE publications department to find out about specific information for parents.

Tel: 0370 000 2288
www.education.gov.uk

Department of Health Publications

www.gov.uk/government/publications

Faith in Families (formerly Catholic Children's Society (Nottingham))

7 Colwick Road, West Bridgford
Nottingham NG2 5FR
Tel: 0115 955 8811
email: enquiries@faithinfamilies.org
www.faithinfamilies.org

Family Futures Consortium Ltd

An adoption and adoption support agency, which specialises in therapeutic work for children who have experienced early trauma and who have attachment difficulties.

3 & 4 Floral Place
7–9 Northampton Grove
London N1 2PL
Tel: 020 7354 4161 (Parent advice line)
email: contact@familyfutures.co.uk
www.familyfutures.co.uk

Family Rights Group (FRG)

A national organisation that advises families who are in contact with social services, about the care of their children.

The Print House, 18 Ashwin Street
London E8 3DL
Tel: 0808 801 0366 (Advice line)
email: advice@frg.org.uk
www.frg.org.uk

First4Adoption

An information service for people interested in adopting a child from England.
www.first4adoption.org.uk

Fostering Network

Provides support and information for foster carers to ensure that all children who are fostered receive the highest standards of care.

87 Blackfriars Road, London SE1 8HA
Tel: 020 7620 6400
email: info@fostering.net
www.fostering.net

Scotland office

2nd Floor, Ingram House
227 Ingram Street, Glasgow G1 1DA
Tel: 0141 204 1400
email: scotland@fostering.net
www.fostering.net

Wales office

1 Caspian Point
Pierhead Street
Cardiff Bay
Cardiff CF10 4DQ
Tel: 029 2044 0940
email: wales@fostering.net

Northern Ireland

Unit 10, 40 Montgomery Road
Belfast BT6 9HL
Tel: 028 9070 5056
email: ni@fostering.net

General Register Office for Northern Ireland

Colby House
Stranmills Ct.
Belfast BT9 5RR
Tel: 0300 200 7890
www.nidirect.gov.uk/gro

Health and Care Professions Council (HCPC) (formerly General Social Care Council (GSCC))

Regulatory body for the social care profession in England.

Park House
184 Kennington Park Road
London SE11 4BU
Tel: 0845 300 6184
www.hcpc-uk.org

Home Education Advisory Service (HEAS)

A UK-based national charity providing information and support for home education. Produces information, provides support for parents, works with LEAs to monitor and inspect home education programmes.

PO Box 98, Welwyn Garden City
Hertfordshire AL8 6AN
Tel: 01707 371 854
email: enquiries@heas.org.uk
www.heas.org.uk

Independent Panel for Special Education Advice (IPSEA)

A charity that aims to ensure that children with special educational needs receive the special education provision to which they are legally entitled. Provides free, independent advice; free advice on appealing to the Special Educational Needs Tribunal (including representation, if needed); second opinions from professionals.

24–26 Gold Street
Saffron Walden CB10 1SJ
www.ipsea.org.uk

Independent Review Mechanism (IRM)

Reviews adoption and fostering suitability applications from prospective and current carers whose agency has decided not to approve them.

Unit 4, Pavilion Business Park
Royds Hall Road
Wortley
Leeds LS12 6AJ
Tel: 0845 450 3956
www.independentreviewmechanism.org.uk

Independent Review Mechanism (IRM) Cymru

25 Windsor Place
Cardiff CF10 3BZ
Tel: 029 2034 2434
www.irm.cymru

The Institute for Arts in Therapy and Education

A college of higher education dedicated to in-depth theoretical and practical study of artistic, imaginative and emotional expression and understanding and enhancement of emotional well-being.

2–18 Britannia Row, London N1 8PA
Tel: 020 7704 2534
email: info@artspsychotherapy.org
www.artspsychotherapy.org

The Institute for Neuro-phsyiological Psychology (INPP)

Established in 1975 to research the effects of central nervous system dysfunction on learning difficulties in children and on adults suffering from neuroses. The institute provides detailed information about this topic and about its services on its website or via post.

1 Stanley Street, Chester CH1 2LR
Tel: 01244 311 414
www.inpp.org.uk

Institute of Child Health

Works in partnership with the Great Ormond Street Hospital to form the largest paediatric training and research centre in the UK. The hospital offers the widest range of paediatric specialists in the country.

30 Guilford Street, London WC1N 1EH
Tel: 020 7242 9789
www.ucl.ac.uk/ich

Intercountry Adoption Centre (IAC)

The only specialist centre for intercountry adoption in the UK, it offers confidential information and advice service for intercountry adopters at any stage of adoption or post adoption. Services include an advice line; counselling for families or for young people who were adopted from overseas; training for professionals involved in adoption; and consultation days for prospective intercountry adopters.

22 Union Street, Barnet
Hertfordshire EN5 4HZ
Tel: 020 8447 4753 (Advice line)
email: info@icacentre.org.uk
www.icacentre.org.uk

Link Maker

Link Maker joins up children's social care across the UK to increase placement choice for children, and to improve use of data and collaboration between local authorities and providers.

St Nicholas House

31–34 High Street
Bristol BS1 2AW
Tel: 0843 886 0040
Email: support@linkmaker.co.uk
www.linkmaker.co.uk

The Mental Health Foundation

Provides information and support for people
and families who have any type of mental health
problem and/or learning disability. Included
within the MHF is The Foundation for People
with Learning Disabilities.

Colechurch House
1 London Bridge Walk
London SE1 2SX
Tel: 020 7803 1100
www.mentalhealth.org.uk

Scotland office

Merchants House
30 George Square, Glasgow G2 1EG
Tel: 0141 572 0145
www.mentalhealth.org.uk

Wales office

Castle Court
6 Cathedral Road
Cardiff CF11 9LJ
Tel: 0921 679 400

Mind

Promotes greater understanding of depression
to reduce the stigma associated with it.
Produces a free booklet, 'The Young Person's
Guide to Stress'.

15–19 Broadway, Stratford
London E15 4BQ
email: supporterservices@mind.org.uk
www.mind.org.uk

National Association for Special Educational Needs (NASEN)

Promotes the education, training, advancement
and development of people with special
educational needs. Services to members include
several regular publications, and regional
courses and conferences.

4–5 Amber Business Village
Amber Close, Amington
Tamworth B77 4RP
Tel: 01827 311 500
email: welcome@nasen.org.uk
www.nasen.org.uk

National Children's Bureau

Promotes the well-being of children in every
aspect of life. Participates in research and policy
development, and provides an information
service, publications and training.

8 Wakley Street, London EC1V 7QE
Tel: 020 7843 6000
email: enquiries@ncb.org.uk
www.ncb.org.uk

Children in Scotland

Tel: 0131 228 8484
email: info@childreninscotland.org.uk

Children in Wales

Tel: 029 2034 2434
email: info@childreninwales.org.uk

National Society for the Prevention of Cruelty to Children (NSPCC)

Provides information and training, in addition to
campaign and policy work to prevent abuse of
children.

Weston House, 42 Curtain Road
London EC2A 3NH
Helpline: 0808 800 5000
www.nspcc.org.uk

New Family Social

A UK charity for lesbian, gay, bisexual and
transgender adopters, foster carers and their
children. It provides advice and information, a
vibrant messageboard, as well as social events
for parents and children to get together.

Harvey's Barn
Park End, Swaffham
Bulbeck CB25 0NA
Tel: 0843 289 9457
www.newfamilysocial.org.uk

Office of Public Sector Information (OPSI)

National Archives
Kew, Richmond
Surrey TW9 4DU
email: legislation@nationalarchives.gsi.gov.uk
www.legislation.gov.uk

Centre for Adoption Support and Education

A centre that provides support for families who adopt. Offers workshops, activities, consultations, networking opportunities.

162 Pennywell Road, Easton
Bristol B55 0TX
Tel: 0117 955 8826
email: info@adoptionsupportcentre.org
www.adoptionsupportcentre.org

Family Lives

Confidential helpline provides information and emotional support to parents.

Tel: 0808 800 2222
www.familylives.org.uk

Positive Parenting Publications and Programmes

Provides information, resources and training for parents and those who support them.

Garth House
Leon Avenue
Cardiff Cf15 7RG
Tel: 0845 643 1939
email:mail@cff.org.uk
www.careforthefamily.org.uk

Post-adoption and adoption support services

Please see Section 5 of this handbook.

School Health Service

Identifies and assesses children who have physical, emotional or behavioural problems. It includes a named school nurse and paediatric doctors who have additional training to help with school services. The Health Service provides advice to LEAs and offers specialist services, such as enuresis (bedwetting) clinics, audiology services, and support/ advice for families and children with physical and emotional difficulties. Contact your local authority or LEA to find phone numbers for your local School Health Teams.

Scottish Health on the Web (SHOW)

Provided by the NHS in Scotland, this site provides general health information, contact details of all NHS Trusts, and links to other websites.

www.show.scot.nhs.uk

Social, Emotional and Behavioural Difficulties Association (SEBDA)

Promotes services for children and young people who have emotional and behavioural difficulties, and supports professionals working with young people. Produces journal, *Emotional and Behavioural Difficulties*, that provides a variety of articles written mainly by professionals in the field. The journal is available from SAGE Publications.

SEBDA
c/o Goldwyn School
Godinton Lane, Great Chart
Ashford, Kent TN23 3BT
email: admin@sebda.org
www.sebda.org

Special Education Consortium

See contact details for Council for Disabled Children.

Stonewall Information Service

Provides information, advice and resources for LGBT+ communities, and works with a range of organisations to help campaign for equality.

Stonewall Parenting
Tower Building, York Road
London SE1 7NX
Tel: 0800 050 2020
email: info@stonewall.org.uk
www.stonewall.org.uk

TalkAdoption

A support programme for young people (to 25 years old) who have a link with adoption, whether adoptee, friend or relative, including a free, confidential helpline.

Tel: 0808 808 1234
Email: talkadoption@afteradoption.org.uk
www.afteradoption.org.uk

Become

Promotes services for children and young people in public care and those who have left public care. Publishes 'Become' magazine.

15–18 White Lion Street
London N1 9PG
Tel: 020 7251 3117
email: advice@becomecharity.org.uk
www.becomecharity.org.uk

UK Youth

A network of organisations dedicated to supporting young people to realise their potential. Delivers and supports high-quality voluntary work and informal education for young people. Provides publications for young people and youth workers about emotional/behavioural issues.

483 Liverpool Road
London N7 8PG
Tel: 020 3137 3810
email: info@ukyouth.org
www.ukyouth.org

United Kingdom Council for Psychotherapy (UKCP)

Holds national register of psychotherapists and gives details of local psychotherapists and counsellors.

America House
2 America Square
London EC3N 2LU
Tel: 020 7014 9955
email:info@ukcp.org.uk
www.psychotherapy.org.uk

YoungMinds: the children's mental health charity

The national charity committed to improving the mental health of all children and young people. Produces a variety of information about many mental health issues, including 'YoungMinds Magazine'. Provides a consultancy service; works with health, education and social services, and the voluntary sector to develop services for children with mental health problems.

Suite 11, Baden Place
Crosby Row
London SE1 1YW
Tel: 020 7089 5050
www.youngminds.org.uk

YoungMinds Parents' Information Service

A telephone service providing information and advice for anyone with concerns about the mental health of a child or young person.

Helpline: 0808 802 5544
www.youngminds.org.uk/for_parents

Youth Access

The largest provider of free and confidential youth counselling and information centres throughout the UK. You can find your local service on:
www.youthaccess.org.uk

1–2 Taylor's Yard
67 Alderbook Road
London SW12 8AD
Tel: 020 8772 9900
email: admin@youthaccess.org.uk

Appendix 3:
National Minimum Standards (NMS) applicable to the provision of adoption services

General Introduction

The National Minimum Standards (NMS) together with the adoption regulations form the basis of the regulatory framework under the Care Standards Act 2000 for the conduct of adoption agencies and adoption support agencies.

The values statement below explains the important principles which underpin these Standards.

Values – children

- The child's welfare, safety and needs are at the centre of the adoption process.

- Adopted children should have an enjoyable childhood, and benefit from excellent parenting and education, enjoying a wide range of opportunities to develop their talents and skills leading to a successful adult life.

- Children are entitled to grow up as part of a loving family that can meet their developmental needs during childhood and beyond.

- Children's wishes and feelings are important and will be actively sought and fully taken into account at all stages of the adoption process.

- Delays should be avoided as they can have a severe impact on the health and development of the children waiting to be adopted.

- A sense of identity is important to a child's well-being. To help children develop this, their ethnic origin, cultural background, religion, language and sexuality need to be properly recognised and positively valued and promoted.

- The particular needs of disabled children and children with complex needs will be fully recognised and taken into account.

- Where a child cannot be cared for in a suitable manner in their own country, intercountry adoption may be considered as an alternative means of providing a permanent family.

- Children, birth parents/guardians and families and adoptive parents and families will be valued and respected.

- A genuine partnership between all those involved in adoption is essential for the NMS to deliver the best outcomes for children; this includes the Government, local government, other statutory agencies, Voluntary Adoption Agencies and Adoption Support Agencies.

Values – adopted adults and birth relatives

- Adoption is an evolving life-long process for all those involved – adopted adults, and birth and adoptive relatives. The fundamental issues raised by adoption may reverberate and resurface at different times and stages throughout an individual's life.

- Adopted people should have access to information and services to enable them to address adoption-related matters throughout their life.

- Agencies have a duty to provide services that considers the welfare of all parties involved and should consider the implications of decisions and actions for everyone involved.

- Agencies should seek to work in partnership with all parties involved, taking account of their views and wishes in decision-making.

- Agencies should acknowledge differences in people's circumstances and establish policies that provide non-discriminatory services.

- Adopted adults have their adoptive identity safeguarded and the right to decide whether to be involved in contact or communication with birth family members.

The detailed standards are the basis for expected outcomes. These outcomes include the following:

- Children know that their views, wishes and feelings are taken into account in all aspects of their care; are helped to understand why it may not be possible to act upon their wishes in all cases; and know how to obtain support and make a complaint.

- Children have a positive self view, emotional resilience and knowledge and understanding of their background.

- Children enjoy sound relationships with their prospective adopters, interact positively with others and behave appropriately.

- Children feel safe and are safe; children understand how to protect themselves and are protected from significant harm including neglect, abuse and accident.

- Children live in a healthy environment where their physical, emotional and psychological health is promoted and where they are able to access the services they need to meet their health needs.

- Children are able to enjoy their interests, develop confidence in their skills and are supported and encouraged to engage in leisure activities.

- The education and achievements of children is actively promoted as valuable in itself and as part of their preparation for adulthood. Children are supported to achieve their educational potential.

- Contact with birth parents, siblings, other members of the birth family and significant others is arranged and maintained when it is beneficial to the child.

- Children live with prospective adopters whose home provides adequate space to a suitable standard. The child enjoys access to a range of activities which promote their development.

- The adoption agency approves adopters who can meet most of the needs of looked after children who are to be placed for adoption and who can provide them with a home where the child will feel loved, safe and secure.

- Children have clear and appropriate information about themselves, their birth parents and families, and life before their adoption.

- Birth parents and birth families take an active part in the planning and implementation of their child's adoption.

- Children benefit from stable placements and are matched and placed with prospective adopters who can meet most, if not all, of their assessed needs.

- Children feel loved, safe and secure with their prospective adoptive parents with whom they were originally placed; and these children were placed within 12 months of the decision of the agency's decision-maker that they should be placed for adoption.

- Children and adults affected by adoption receive an assessment of their adoption support needs.

- Service users confirm that the adoption support services provided met or are meeting their assessed needs.

- Adopted adults and birth relatives are assisted to obtain information in relation to the adoption, where appropriate, and contact is facilitated between an adopted adult and their birth relative if that is what both parties want.

- The adoption panel and decision-maker make timely, quality and appropriate recommendations/ decisions in line with the overriding objective to promote the welfare of children throughout their lives.

Where there are changes, these are noted under the headings in *Effective Panels* with page references. There is a section in the introduction to the Guidance – para 5, 'Making the adoption process work well' – which is included here, in summary.

Reproduced from *Adoption: National Minimum Standards*, Department for Education, 2011. This information is licensed under the terms of the Open Government Licence (www.education.gov.uk/publications/eOrderingDownload/Adoption–NMS.pdf accessed 14/11/2011)

Appendix 4:
The Adoption Passport

The adoption passport: a support guide for adopters

Children adopted from care can have ongoing needs, and you and your child may benefit from support. This is the support adopters in England may be entitled to:

For your child...

Children adopted from care have priority access to schools, which means that your child should be able to attend whichever school you think best meets their needs (www.gov.uk/schools-admissions). From September 2014, they will also be entitled to free early education from the age of two (tinyurl.com/first4early).

If your child needs extra support, you can ask your local authority to assess their needs for adoption support services (see page 2). If you think your child may have special educational needs you can ask your local authority to assess these needs too.

For you as an adopter...

Many adopters are entitled to adoption leave and pay when their child is placed with them (www.gov.uk/adoption-pay-leave). The law is changing to make this entitlement more similar to maternity and paternity leave pay, and it will include the right to take time off when you are meeting your child, before they move in with you.

Adopters may have priority for council housing (www.gov.uk/council-housing). If you are living in council housing and claiming Housing Benefit or Universal Credit while waiting for a child to move in you can also apply for funding (Discretionary Housing Payments) so that you are not penalised financially while you have an empty spare room.

You are also entitled to a summary of your child's health from his or her local authority's medical adviser before he or she is placed with you, and to a life-story book to help your child understand his or her early life.

Adoption Support Services

Local authorities provide and fund a range of support services for children adopted from care. These support services can include:

- counselling, information and advice
- help with behavioural, attachment and other problems
- money e.g. to help with special care needs, or for former foster parents
- help with contact between an adopted child and his or her birth family
- meetings and events to enable groups of adopters and adoptive children to get together
- training to help adopters to meet the needs of their adoptive child
- short breaks for an adopted child with another carer
- help where an adoption breaks down.

Access to these services depends on your circumstances but you can ask for an assessment *at any time*, no matter how long after the adoption.

Support Services Advice

Your local authority will have an Adoption Support Services Adviser to help you access adoption support and other specialist services, such as Child and Adolescent Mental Health Services. The NHS commissions health services to meet the needs of adopted children, and the National Institute for Health and Care Excellence will produce new guidance so that your GP will understand the problems you may face. The Adoption Support Services Adviser's details should be available on the local authority's website.

Every adopter is entitled to an assessment of their adoption support needs, but local authorities do not have to provide support in response to an assessment. Which services you are able to access will depend on your circumstances. Future changes to the law will mean that local authorities must tell adopters about adoption support services and their right to an assessment, and will give those who receive support a choice about how that support is provided, either by a local authority or through a 'personal budget' to purchase services from a voluntary adoption agency or adoption support agency.

If you want advice on adoption support you can also contact one of the many adoption support organisations, such as Adoption UK (www.adoptionuk.org.uk) or the British Association for Adoption and Fostering (www.baaf.org.uk), or read the e learning materials soon to be on the First4Adoption web-site which will explore the effect of children's experiences on their development and the services available to help them.

Which local authority?

The local authority that places the child with you is responsible for assessing your adoption support needs for three years after the adoption. After three years it becomes the responsibility of the local authority where you live (if different).

Comments and complaints

If you are unhappy with the support provided by your local authority, or with the time taken to carry out an assessment, you can complain under the Local Authority Complaints Procedure. Thereafter if you are not satisfied you may be able to refer your complaint to the Local Government Ombudsman (www.lgo.org.uk). You will also soon be able to raise general concerns with the new Champion for adopters, foster carers and special guardians.

FIRST 4 ADOPTION is the dedicated information service for anyone interested in adopting a child in England. It is managed by Coram Children's Legal Centre, Coram and Adoption UK, and supported and funded by the Department for Education.

- Call First4Adoption: 0300 222 0022
- Visit our website: first4adoption.org.uk
- Follow us on Twitter: @First4Adoption

Supported by

Department for Education

© Crown copyright 2013

Index

Abuse, effects on child 96–111

Adoption Registers 32–4

Adoption, talking about with your child 121–24

Adoption allowance 77

Adoption and Children Act 2002 35, 43, 50, 52, 58, 60, 61, 72, 124

Adoption centres 71

Adoption certificate 47

Adoption leave 44–46, 80

Adoption Match 12, 15, 141

Adoption Order 16, 21, 43, 47, 60, 66, 72, 74
applying for 59, 64, 66, 68, 69–70, 75

Adoption panel 22–23
approval by 25–28

Adoption passport 51, 124

Adoption placement order (see Placement order)

Adoption process 10–13, 18–55

Adoptive parents, legal requirements and entitlements 65–66

Adoption Support Fund 55, 56, 107, 111, 129

Approval (see Adoption panel) 25–28

Assessment (see Home study) 22–25

Attention Deficit Hyperactivity Disorder 102–4

Attachment difficulties 101–2

Bed wetting 98, 128

Birth parents, legal requirements and entitlements 66–67

Care Order 60

Carer's allowance 141

Certificate of Approval 53

Children's guardian 42, 61, 71, 76

Child's Permanence Report 28

Community health services for children 104

Complaints 29, 79

Concurrent planning 19–20

Contact, in adoption 35, 37, 38, 41, 42–44, 51

Contact Order 61

Couple relationship 127

Court fees 75

Courts, requirement to attend role in adoption process 72

Criminal offences, prohibiting adoption 22

Culture and ethnicity, of child 27, 36

Developmental delay 98–101

Directions hearings 72

Disability Living Allowance (DLA) 80

Disabled children 80, 109–110

Disruption 42, 125
and eligibility to adopt again 19
handling emotions 125

Domicile 16

Education, child's educational history 31, 82–94

Emergency protection order 61

Emotional needs, children 106–109, 112–114
parents 9, 116–118

Encopresis (see Soiling)

Enuresis (see Bed wetting)

Final hearing 72

Finances, adoption costs 75–80
assistance with 75–80

Foster carers, as adopters 16–17

Fostering allowance 77

Fostering for adoption 20

Gay couples, as adoptive parents 16, 19

Grandparents, as adopters 17–19

Health and Care Professions Council 12, 25

Health issues 31–32, 54, 95–114

Health visitor 44, 98, 99, 103, 104

Home study 25, 53

Independent Review Mechanism 19, 30

Independent school 85, 87

Individual Education Plan (IEP) 85

Intercountry adoption 51–55

Intermediary services 50

Introductions, to child 39–40

Later life letter 42

Learning Support Unit (LSU) 85

Legal fees, in adoption 75

Lesbian couples, as adoptive parents 16, 19

Life story book 42, 106

Link Maker 12, 15, 28, 32, 36, 146

Linking 28

Maternity leave (see Adoption leave)

Medical history, child's 28, 31–32
    prospective adopter's 27

Neglect, effects on child 10, 54, 96–114

Overseas adoption (see Intercountry adoption)

Parental leave (see Adoption leave)

Parental responsibility 47, 62

Parents, adoptive, meeting needs of 116–129

Paternity leave (see Adoption leave)

Physiotherapy 104

Placement, of child with adopters 40

Placement orders 62

Post-adoption services and support 50–51, 54

Post-placement support 50–51

Post-traumatic stress disorder 102

Prospective adopters, legal requirements and
    entitlements 65–66

Prospective Adopters' Report 25

Protection of Children Act 1999 58

Pupil Premium 84, 87, 88

"Race" 27

Reporting Officer 42, 62, 70

Religion, of child 34–36

Residence order 6, 7, 63

Rights, adopter's 24–25
    children's 6

Schooling (see Education)

Settling-in grant 41

Siblings 37

Single parents, as adopters 19

Social networking and contact 51

Social workers 12, 47, 49, 117

Soiling 98, 128

Special Educational Needs (SEN) 86–94
    Co-ordinator (SENCo) 86

SEN Code of Practice 2000 90
    Statement of 90
    Tribunal 90

Special guardianship 17, 63

Supervision order 63

Therapy 31, 76, 104

Trauma, effects on child 54, 96–114

Unmarried couples, as adopters 19

Voluntary adoption agencies 12

Read about adoption!

These real-life stories explore the highs and lows of adoption. Written by adopters and carers, they reveal the hard times and happy times, the waiting and hoping, the setbacks and disappointments, and the absolute joy of adopting a child!

Jayne Lilley

Nicola Hill

Julia Wise

Laurel Ashton

Robert Marsden

Mike Butcher

Jules Belle

RUBY CLAY

Pablo Fernández

To find out more visit www.corambaaf.org.uk/bookshop

PARENTING MATTERS

This unique series provides expert knowledge about a range of children's health conditions, coupled with facts, figures and guidance presented in a straightforward and accessible style. Adopters and foster carers also describe what it is like to parent an affected child, "telling it like it is", sharing their parenting experiences and offering useful advice.

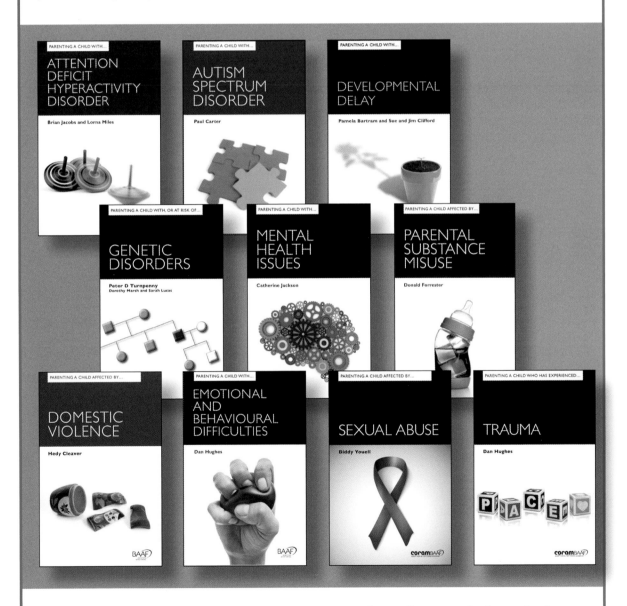

To find out more visit www.corambaaf.org.uk/bookshop